Grace Has Been Granted

A Journey Through Grief

Jeff Harrelson

Contents

Introduction

"My grace is sufficient for you, for my power is made perfect in weakness"
2 Corinthians 12:9

What a journey my family and I have been on since Sept. 14, 2020. A journey that we never would have expected or chosen. We have learned about grace. God's grace. His unmerited favor towards His people. We have learned through our trials that God has a plan. Even if we don't understand it. We often don't know the full plan. Sometimes he only shows it to us in part. What we do know in part, however, is always sufficient. What we now know in part, we will also one day know in full.

The beginning of the Harrelson 6, as we often refer to ourselves as, began back in 1995 when I attended a Sunday school party at the home of Robin and Greg Madden. Robin and I sang together in the choir at Taylors First Baptist Church. I had no idea that attending the same party would be Kara Block who worked with Robin at Slater-Marietta Elementary School. Kara and I met for the first time that night. Long story short, we were engaged six months later. And then in the summer of 1996, we became Mr. and Mrs. Harrelson. Robin knew what she was doing. In 2000, we became the Harrelson 3 as our daughter Callie Jane was born. In 2002, we became the Harrelson 4 as our son Jacob Allen was born. In 2003, we became the Harrelson 5 as our second son Grant Edward was born. We remained the Harrelson 5 for seven more years. Then in 2010, the Harrelson 6 became complete with the birth of Zackary Carl.

I am currently a math teacher and basketball coach at Pickens High School. Kara is the assistant principal at Northwest Crescent Child Development Center. Callie is a recent graduate at Clemson University where Jake still attends Clemson. Callie is a first year teacher at Eastside High School, my alma mater. Zack is starting middle school at League Academy in the sixth gradel. Grant would've been beginning his freshman year of college. We still attend Taylors First Baptist Church.

We had no idea that in September of 2020 we would tragically and unexpectedly lose our son and third child Grant Edward Harrelson. But God knew. At the end of the day, even through the questioning and wrestling with God over the "why", we have learned to trust Him. During the days after his accident and subsequent passing, I began writing. I am by no means a writer. I am a math teacher. Totally different part of the brain. Nonetheless, part of my grieving process was to write down my thoughts. I posted many of them on Facebook. I received lots of feedback and prayers. Many people told me I should write a devotional book. I kind of laughed them off. That sounded impossible to me. Again, I'm not a writer. As the months passed, I still felt like God was speaking to me and teaching me more about Him. This is my attempt at a book. It is a collection of posts from Facebook (in italics) with some personal reflections looking back over the past twenty months. If it helps one person deal with the grief of losing a child or loved one then it will have been well worth my time. This is Grant's story. This is a grieving father's story. But in the end , this is a story about God and how his strength begins when ours comes to an end. Grace that only He can grant.

Pressure Washers

September 12, 2020: "Does anyone know someone who works on pressure washers?"

September 15, 2020: "Need urgent prayer"

These were two Facebook posts of mine within a few days of each other. I've included the first one just as a reminder that your world can go from ordinary and normal to upside down in just a moment. I sent the second one from Greenville Memorial Hospital after midnight when Kara and I arrived at the emergency room.

Monday, September 14, 2020 seemed just like a normal day in the Harrelson household. We had just moved Jake into his freshman dorm at Clemson just a few days before. Callie was already in her apartment at Clemson about to begin her junior year. Kara and I both worked that day. Grant and Zack were home since that was their virtual day that week. We had such a great dinner that night with great conversation. Later that evening, we went to bed not knowing what the next 36 hours would entail for our family.

At 1:00 am, our doorbell rang. I don't even believe I heard it, but Kara was awakened. Once she got up, I woke up dazed and confused. Kara walked downstairs and could hear her parents outside of our front door. They told us that Grant and Parker, his cousin, had been involved in a car accident and were headed to the hospital. Kara and I both looked at each other thinking that was impossible. Of course Grant was downstairs in his bed. Kara went downstairs and found that he was not there.

We got in the car and headed towards the hospital, not knowing what we would find once we got there. When we got to the ER, I started yelling, "where's Grant Harrelson?" At first, no one could tell me. You see, he did not have any ID on him that night. According to the hospital, he was known as "New Mexico". They assign names to people who are unresponsive and without identification. Thankfully, the ER chaplain was able to meet us and take us to a waiting room. We met with the police briefly. Grant had not been wearing a seat belt. The car he was in flipped several times and he was ejected. He had to be revived at the scene once the paramedics arrived. We also learned that Emma, a friend, had also been a passenger in the car and had been ejected as well. Parker had been wearing a seatbelt and was not ejected from the car but was cut up pretty bad. Not long after Grant arrived at the ER, he was taken to the Neuro ICU with a brain injury.

September, 15, 2020: "Please pray for our son Grant. He was involved in a very serious car accident last night. He's in the Neuro ICU in critical condition. We thank you for all of the prayers so far. Please continue to pray that the Great Healer will lay His hands upon him and heal his body"

The next 36 hours seemed like years. The waiting and the unknown were crippling. All the while God gave us gentle reminders that He was in control. The hospital went against policy and allowed both Kara and me in Grant's room. Students began gathering outside the hospital to just pray for Grant, Emma and Parker and be there for each other. Looking out of the hospital window above and seeing all of their friends and classmates was a blessing. Our church held a prayer vigil for them on that Tuesday night. We watched it remotely from the hospital. I learned that a student of mine, Mackenzie, had started a GoFundMe account for our family. Our church created a "Pray for Grant" Facebook profile picture that many people posted.

We met with the neurologist that Tuesday night and did not get great news. He said Grant's injuries were very severe. It was tough news to hear but we were not through praying and believing that Grant would walk out of that hospital. Because of his age, the neurologist would perform two tests for brain activity. They had to be 24 hours apart so we continued to wait. I began creating a playlist of songs called "Fly High Grant". It became therapy for me. What started as one song grew to over 6 hours of songs. One of the first songs I chose was "Even If" by Casting Crowns. It basically says that God had the power to save Grant if he chose. We would still love and trust Him if he chose not to, however.

September 16, 2020: "No change in Grant's condition. We need a miracle. Please keep praying for our family. Grant's final neurological test is set for 10:00 pm tonight. Please pray that God would perform a miracle and Grant would show signs of brain activity."

Once again, all we could do was wait. Despite our feelings of sadness and despair, Kara and I both felt such a calm and peace throughout the day. We were fully confident and expectant that Grant would pull through. We prayed over, sang over and just talked to him all day. We kept waiting for him to squeeze our hands. As 10:00 pm came, we were quite anxious but at ease. At 10:15 pm, the neurologist looked at us and told us the news we did not want to hear. I will be totally transparent. We felt totally abandoned by God and lost in that moment. We were drained physically, emotionally and spiritually. One of the darkest moments in our family's lives. We went home that evening from the hospital. What do we do now? Where do we go from here? Looking back, we now realize that the only way Grant could be completely healed was in the presence of Jesus.

September 17, 2020: "Last night we lost our sweet son Grant. In the end, his brain injury was too severe to overcome. We have been amazed at the overwhelming outpouring of love and support for Grant and our family during this time. We could not have gone through this dark time without it. Our family is heartbroken but we know he is in a better place right now and has been healed and made whole again. We firmly believe that God is in control even when our lives seem out of control. We will praise Him in this valley. Please continue to pray for our family as we navigate these difficult days."

That has to be one of the toughest things I have ever had to write. Well, at least for a few days. I can't imagine going through Grant's accident without God. In our despair, we still praised God for a couple of things. First, the neurologist assured us that it was likely that Grant felt no pain. Second, we were able to spend 36 hours by his side. Those are moments we will always remember and cherish. Later that day we met with the organ donation team. We were able to read comments and posts from his classmates at Wade Hampton High School. Even though we felt the world crumbling under our feet, God kept reminding us that it was going to be okay.

So when you feel like your heart has been ripped out and that God has somehow forgotten about you, how do you still have the confidence to pray? **Mark 11:24 says, "Therefore, I tell you, whatever you ask for in prayer, believe that you have received it and it will be yours."** We prayed and we believed but we did not get the answer that we wanted. When God gives you a "no" or a "not yet" answer to your prayer it is easy to question your faith. Is God just ignoring us? If God is sovereign, then why even pray at all? Can God be persuaded to change His mind or alter His plans? If not, what's the point? I have learned that prayer is not about results, it is about a relationship. We should not use prayer as a spiritual vending machine, only using it when we need something. We were created to have a relationship with Him. He wants us to come to Him at all times both good and bad. He can handle our cries of desperation and doubt. He desires to wrestle with us over our trials. David and Job are two great examples of this. Who are we to tell God what He needs to do in our life? He doesn't owe us anything. We owe Him everything.

I really struggled with the idea that a parent should not outlive a child. It's just not the natural order of life. It's at this point that I really began to question God and His purposes. But He was right there to reassure me that Grant was in good hands now, the best hands, and that his life would not end in vain.

September 18, 2020: "These past few days still seem like a bad dream. Our family has been on a roller coaster ride of emotions. Our faith in God and our friends have held us up and sustained us. We praise God that he is now healed and has been made whole again. We had prayed for a miracle for God to heal him. We now know that the only way he could be healed was to be in the presence of Jesus. Our hope on this day is that the miracle that we prayed for could be seen in the life of someone else through Grant's organs. The kind words spoken about Grant from his friends, teammates and classmates have been a ray of sunshine in the darkness. We love all of you. *"He will wipe away every tear from their eyes, and death shall be no more, neither shall there be mourning, nor crying, nor pain anymore, for the former things have passed away." Revelations 21:4*

September 19, 2020: "I woke up this morning just thinking about Grant. Early quiet mornings and late nights have been the toughest. A lot of people have told us that they can't imagine what we're going through. At times we can't imagine it. But today instead of pain and sadness we choose joy. I sat down and went back and listened to our pastor Dr. Allen McWhite's sermon from last week. It was entitled "When the lights seem like they're going out". It was not his original, intended message that he had prepared. God laid this one on his heart at the last moment. Only God knew how much we would need these words of encouragement from this message.

1. Faith accepts - There will be pain and loss in this world. Suffering colors life but we get to choose the color.

*2. Faith adheres- It holds on and clings to God. We will not reach any conclusion from this tragedy until God is through with it. **Philippians 1:6 sys,"I am sure of this, that He who started a good work in you will carry it on to the completion until the day of Christ Jesus"***

3. Faith anticipates- Death, pain and suffering don't have the final word. Through Christ, we have already won.

We know that there will still be more times of tears and sadness but we cling to the fact that God is with us. Today we choose joy. We pray that you will find that light in the darkness and that joy in the pain. Our joy is that our family has hugged more, loved more, prayed more and supported each other more. I pray this will be a reminder for your family to do the same. Grant's in a better place and he's just waiting on us. "

I really debated going to church this Sunday. Everyone would've understood. In the end, I just felt that I needed to be there. Callie went with me. Dr. McWhite even acknowledged our presence in the service (even though he mistakenly thought Callie was Kara. We were sitting in the back however) I thought it was definitely a God thing when we walked into the service and sat across the aisle from Jay and Kim Weaver. Their son Andrew had died tragically a few years prior. I'm glad we went.

Dr. McWhite would continue to be such a tremendous support to our family. His constant texts and prayers were such an encouragement to us. Several months later our church would call our next pastor, Josh Powell, who has also been such a blessing to our family. We attend and serve in a tremendous church, Taylors First Baptist Church.

September 20, 2020: " God is good. All the time. What a wonderful Sunday. We have prayed really hard that Grant's organs would be viable and be able to be donated. We received a phone call early this morning that Grant's heart, liver and both kidneys would be able to be used to give someone else life. God took our prayer for 1 miracle and multiplied it by 4. God's mercies are new every morning. Grant's legacy will live on through the gift of his body. Praise God. He is good. "Because of the Lord's great love we are not consumed, for his compassions never fail. They are new every morning; great is your faithfulness." Lamentations 3:22-23

The next week for our family was quite a wild ride of emotions. Sunday morning we got the call about Grant's organs being viable. By Sunday afternoon, they had already been transplanted. It happened so fast. Fox 21 came by the house to interview us about Grant's story. It went so well. Just as we had prayed that it would. But then we also had to deal with the reality of writing Grant's obituary and planning his service.

September 21, 2020: "This morning Kara, Callie, Zack and I were lying in bed together (Jake went back to Clemson and no... we did not all sleep in the same bed last night). We realized that today was the last day of summer and that a new season was beginning tomorrow. I immediately thought of Ecclesiastes 3. Seasons and times in our lives constantly change. God is not surprised by any of these changes. Grant's death did not catch him off guard. He knew long before we did that this day was coming. He has promised not to leave us nor forsake us however. Have we been mad at times? Absolutely. Sad? Definitely. Have we questioned Him? Certainly. But we have the hope that even though we don't know "why" right now, one day we will. Thank you Dr. McWhite for reminding us of that yesterday in church. If you're reading this, do you have that hope? We are in the middle of hurricane season. Our family experienced a Category 5 "hurricane" this past week. The ONLY reason our family was not destroyed is our strong foundation in God. He has been our anchor. He will continue to be for the rest of our lives until we see that witty, tall red-headed son of ours. I pray that whatever season of life you are in right now, that you will embrace each season. Love each other more, hold your loved ones tighter, give to others in need. Sometimes seasons change unexpectedly as they have for us. Please reach out to me if you don't have this hope in your life. I would be honored to introduce you to Jesus. Your life will be forever changed."

September 22, 2020: "I never would have imagined that on the morning of September 22, 2020 that I would be writing the obituary for one of my kids. Not something I would choose, obviously, but our ways are not always God's ways. That's never an easy lesson but God has never failed us and He never will. I pray for the Calder family as they are having to do the same things we are having to do this week.

Grant loved basketball. We will miss hearing that ball bounce on our court in the backyard. Kara and I would often lay in bed at night and we could still faintly hear that pounding sound of a basketball. Grant was SO competitive. He was already looking forward to this upcoming basketball season. As a coach, we both always looked forward to a new season that would bring a new confidence and excitement. No matter how the previous season ended, a new season was a reason for fresh hope. We all started undefeated.

Today is the first day of fall. A new start. Fresh expectations. Grant has now started a season where he will always be undefeated. If you know Grant, I'm sure he would not be afraid to tell you that. He always had a little swag. I think his red "flow" gave him his confidence. Our family is still here on earth trying to navigate through our new season. God has not promised us an undefeated season, but He has promised that no matter what comes to our family this new season, that we have already won the prize. He has promised this same to you as well. Why then do we often live like we are defeated? Instead of telling God how big our storms are, we should tell our storms how big our God is. That is true hope that no matter what the world throws at us, we have already won the victory. There will still be tears, questions and confusion in the days ahead but our God is there to pick us up and declare us winners.

Our family continues to earnestly pray that people will come to know Jesus through Grant's death. God is SO good. Why would someone choose to not live in victory? Maybe no one has told them about it or seen it lived out in a believers life. The gift of life that Grant was able to give through his organs is the same gift that we can give to those who don't know Him. We don't need a hospital or medicine to save lives. Just an obedient spirit to share the amazing grace of our Lord Jesus Christ.

Do you know the truth? The truth is that God does not care about the things you have done in the past. If God chose us by our own merits then no one would be worthy of his grace. He is ready to pick you up, wipe you off and give you a new life. Trials will still come in this life but He will never leave you. He will be the anchor that holds you when the winds of life appear. He has been our anchor. We are thankful for His amazing grace. We don't always deserve it but He is faithful and good."

As hard as it was to announce that Grant had passed away, it paled in comparison to writing his obituary. No parent should ever have to go through that.

September 23, 2020: "Behold, Jehovah, seated on the throne. Abba, Father, the well that overflows. The God who was and is and shall be forevermore. Holy is the Lord"

I went to bed last night and woke up this morning just wanting to praise the Lord. Music has been such a source of strength for me this past week. People have been sending us songs that have really ministered to us. It seems like every time I get in the car a song is playing that I either shared with someone or they had shared with me. Coincidence? Hardly. One of Grant's coaches sent me the devotional he read this morning entitled "What happens when you stand up for your faith". It's the story of the fiery furnace in the bible. It says that "Shadrach, Meshach and Abednego didn't know they'd find Jesus in the fire when they walked in the furnace. But they allowed their faith, not fear, to guide their actions (Daniel 2:17-18). Faith rarely makes reasonable sense. So when people see faith in action, they need an explanation."

I have never been much of a "poster" on social media. I hope that my posts have been that "explanation" of our family's faith. God laid it on my heart to speak at Grant's memorial service. At first, I was like "there's no way I can hold it together and do that". But then I thought, "God has strengthened us through this whole situation. I think he's got me on Saturday." These posts of mine have really been kind of a trial run as I have prayed, meditated and read scripture. They are the thoughts that God has sent me. From my closest friends to complete strangers. Isn't it amazing how God works? He knows just what we need. These posts have been helpful to me in the grieving process. I hope they have been helpful and maybe brought a little comfort and encouragement to those that have read them.

We met with the principal at WHHS yesterday just to thank him for his leadership in helping and being there for not only Grant and his friends but the entire student body at WHHS. We talked about how often the "good" gets buried in the headlines. And there is a LOT of good in this world. I could write a book about all the good things, often at unexpected times from unexpected people, that God has provided for our family. It is too bad that it would take a tragedy for us to rally around each other and come together. This should be the story of our lives, not only through the tough times, but the good times as well. This has caused me to be more intentional in my words and actions. Our world has become such a dark and confusing place for so many people. We, as believers, must be that "city on a hill" that shines light. I encourage you today to reach out to that friend that you haven't spoken to in awhile. Call that family member that you might have drifted away from. Grant loved his friends and teammates dearly through thick and thin. He would want us to try to make this world a better place. For we have the only thing that can do that. Jesus."

September 24, 2020: "Let us come into His presence with thanksgiving; let us make a joyful noise to him with songs of praise! For the Lord is a great God, and a great King above all gods." Psalms 95:2-3

It's hard to believe that it's only been a week since Grant went to be with the Lord. It's been hard keeping up with what day it is at times. Our prayers have continually been answered by God. We prayed that God would be the highlight of our news interview last night. He sent a sweet, loving and caring reporter to our house. Things could not have gone any better. That is a God thing. We've seen a lot of those lately. I thought of a couple of things after last night. Our interview wasn't shown until about halfway through the news program. So many evil and negative things preceded it in the broadcast. Unfortunately, that is the world that we live in currently. The good in life gets pushed to the bottom. Seldom is the headline good news. How often do we bury God at the bottom of the page of our life? He should be the headline. He should be the lead story. The world looks at us when tragedy happens. Grant's friends are looking at our family to see how to grieve. I pray that our faith will point them towards God. Our fear was that when God did not "grant" us the miracle that we desired that all of those who had prayed so hard with us would move away from God. A friend of Kara's reminded us that God could handle that. That was on Him. We did not have to carry that burden. We should not expect those who do not know him to respond like those who do. Who in your life is looking at you? What headline do they read when they look at you? I pray that through all of this that we would keep God at his rightful place in our lives. Front and center. The headline. The lead story."

I still think back to that night when God sent us Amber Worthy, Fox 21 reporter. A local newspaper had interviewed us a few days earlier. We were less than impressed with the article. "Grant Harrelson, a tall red head......". So we were a little skeptical when we got the call from Fox. Could we have ever been more wrong. She walked into our living room, looked at a few pictures and began crying. She felt our pain and we could not have been more happier with the final product of the interview. She nailed it.

September 25, 2020: "Enter His gates with thanksgiving and his courts with praise; give thanks to Him and praise His name. For the Lord is good and his love endures forever; his faithfulness continues through all generations." Psalm 100:4-5

Up early this morning, which is unlike me. I've had lots of things over these past two weeks take root in my mind. Most of my posts have focused on our family's journey of grief and recovery. This morning I woke up thinking about what Grant must be experiencing. I'm sure you can remember when you were younger (maybe even currently lol), your parents calling out your name. And if your middle name was attached you knew you had either done or not done something. "Grant, take out the trash." "Grant, time for supper." "Grant, have you done your homework?" Grant Edward Harrelson in no means was a saint. He was a typical 16 year old boy who did typical 16 year old boy things. As many times as he had heard his name called out in our house, he had never quite heard his name called out like he did at 10:16 pm on Wednesday, September 16. He got to hear the creator of the universe, the Lord of the heavens, our heavenly father call out his name and usher him into His presence and glory for eternity. Wow! I can only imagine what that must feel like. God has given us the hope that one day we will experience what that feels like. And Grant will be there with God to invite us in. He just ran ahead a little bit and is there waiting for us."

Needless to say, I didn't sleep much that night in anticipation of the next day. Planning a funeral in 2020 in the midst of a global pandemic was not easy. We were worried about how many people could attend with all of the Covid protocols on gatherings. We were given a max number but luckily our worship minister, Kevin Batson, said if we went over that number then we just went over. He was such a blessing in helping plan with us. We asked all of his friends to wear a jersey in honor of Grant. We were overwhelmed to say the least.

September 26, 2020: The Celebration of Grant Edward Harrelson's life

These are the words that I spoke at Grant's funeral. God definitely got me through it.

"Oh, give thanks to the Lord. For He is good. For His mercy endures forever."
It's really neat to look out and see all of the jerseys being worn. Grant would definitely approve. Maybe not the Clemson ones so much. Zack said just this one time he would wear a FSU jersey. I had Callie convinced that I was going to wear Grant's WH jersey today. She said, "aren't the smaller numbers the smaller sizes?". He was #0. It would not have been a good look and I'm sure Grant would say how ridiculous I looked. He's probably also fussing about having this service on a Saturday because we're messing with Game Day.

Our family had never envisioned this day coming. God knew. His ways are greater than ours. That is often such a hard lesson to learn. You can go from a mountain to a valley in just a moment. But the same God that we rejoice on the top of the mountain is right with us in the valley to pick us up, dust us off and restore us.

On December 5, 2003 we expectantly and joyfully welcomed Grant into this world. On September 16, 2020 we gave him back to God. 16 wonderful years. Full of great memories that we will always remember.

Grant was born into this church. He loved Jesus and he loved this church. Some of his closest friendships from birth were formed within these walls. He accepted Jesus through all of his experiences with this church. He and his friends used to sit right up there on the back row of the balcony during Sunday morning services. Kara and I were constantly texting him, "get off your phone" or "look up and pay attention". Something got through those ears because we have the assurance that he is looking down on all of us this afternoon. He's probably telling me to not talk too long.

Grant loved all sports, especially basketball. One of the biggest things we will miss is watching him play basketball. In preschool, he would throw objects into the sink working on his shot. In elementary school, he bragged that he played on the best church basketball team of all time. In high school, he was proud to be a part of the WHHS basketball program. He loved all of his teammates. And trust me, one day I'm pretty sure he will give you a critique of how you play this upcoming season. We have such great memories of all of the AAU trips with his TR Elite travel team. They knew him as "Hollywood". Grant was my Florida State buddy. I remember us being so excited watching the Noles win the national championship in 2013. Not too much excitement since then, but I figure that Grant now has the ear of God. Maybe we can get a little extra heavenly help this year.

Then there was that hair. The "Flow". Growing up he didn't really like the red hair because of all of the attention it brought. Once he got to high school, he started embracing it. Man did he embrace it. I constantly tried to get him to cut it. He said I was just jealous. Girls would always ask him how he got his hair to be so shiny and clean looking. He always responded, "I wash it". Once he had passed, we asked the nurse if we could cut a lock of his hair. After Kara cut it, I looked down at him and told him , "I told you I would finally cut your hair".

Grant loved his friends SO much. He always told us "People like me. And their parents like me." We would always nod and say okay, whatever. He had a magnetic personality. Many of his friends have posted how much they loved his smile and his ability to make your day better. Those words warmed our hearts. Quarantine was tough on him because our house was a constant revolving door of his friends. I think he and his buddies had a schedule somewhere of who's turn it was to host the sleepover. Our refrigerator would go from full to empty overnight. He loved playing basketball in our backyard with his friends. Losers either had to lay in the creek behind our house in their underwear or get shocked by our dog's shock collar. To look out his hospital room's window and to see all of his friends gathered in front of the hospital praying was a constant reminder to us of how loved he was by his friends. He loved each of you deeply as well.

Our family has experienced the full gamut of emotions through this experience. Have we been angry and mad? Absolutely. Have we been sad? Most certainly. Have we asked God why? For sure. God understands all of them and tells us that we can come to Him and lay our burdens down at his feet. It's not wrong to feel any of those or ask the hard questions. He can handle them.

God did not answer our prayer for a miracle to spare his life. He did answer our prayer for Him to heal him. He is now healed and made whole again in the presence of Jesus. He will continue to live on through the gift of four of his organs. Praise God for that. Our plea for a miracle was multiplied by four. Grant's story is not finished. We still hurt as a family but our hope has never been quenched. God has been so gracious and good to us. He has surrounded us with his love shown through our friends, family and even complete strangers. Our family has come closer together. We have hugged more, loved more and cared more. It shouldn't have taken a tragedy to cause this. I hope our story has been a reminder to all of us to take pause each day to embrace our loved ones and celebrate God's goodness.

We didn't know that on Monday, September 14, that would be the last conversations we would have with Grant. We've been through all of the what if's but we have been reminded that we can't go back and change anything even though we would do whatever it takes to do so. We have to look to the present and to the future. We are not promised tomorrow. So often people say they will get right with God sometime down the road. We are so thankful that Grant made that decision prior to Sept. 16. He got to hear our Heavenly Father call out his name and call him in to spend eternity with Him in heaven. Do you have that same hope? You may be sitting there thinking "God doesn't want me. I've made too many mistakes in life. I'm too far gone. I'm too broken." If it were up to our own merits, then none of us would be worthy. We were created by God to have a relationship with Him. It is through his love and grace that he receives us. We certainly don't deserve it. He promises to heal every scar of your life. He will make every mistake right again. He promises to walk with you through every valley. He throws all of our sins away as far as the east is from the west. He washes us white as snow. Please don't walk out those doors today without having full confidence that Jesus is your Lord. Don't leave this place thinking I'll deal with God later. How wonderful it would be to know today that whenever our time on this earth has passed that God will call out YOUR name and invite you into his presence forever. The hope and love that has sustained our family through Grant's death is available to all who call on his name. It is ONLY through Him that our family has been able to walk through this valley and still lift our hands and praise Him. We have constantly said lately that we could not imagine anyone going through what we have gone through without the loving arms of God. I come back to his jersey. #0. I think it represents so much here today. Grant is in a place with no more pain. No more death. No more loss. No more tears. Grant is undefeated for eternity alongside our God.

"Yes, my soul. Find rest in God; My hope comes from Him. Truly He is my rock and my salvation; He is my fortress, I will not be shaken." Psalms 62:5-6

FLY HIGH GRANT!! We love you and will miss you!

September 26, 2020: " Wow. What a day. We couldn't have been more overjoyed with Grant's service today. We pray that seeds were planted today. We are continually overwhelmed at God's grace and goodness. Kara has continued to amaze me with her strength. As a father I have grieved, but I can only imagine a mother's grief. Her strength through these past few weeks have encouraged me. She is such a strong woman with such a strong faith. I couldn't imagine going through this with anyone else. I love her so much. Grant was so blessed to have such an amazing mother."

Grant's service truly was a celebration of his life. It was the culmination of several weeks of highs and some very tough lows. The love and support of our friends, family, church and community were tremendous. We definitely felt cared for and carried through this tragedy in our life. I remember going to bed that night thinking, "Okay God. What now?" I would learn that our journey of grief was not over with. It was just beginning. The same God who carried us through the first two weeks of this trial would continue to see us through every subsequent moment, both high and low.

So Now What?

September 28, 2020: (Kara's words) "So now what...? Life is continuing. Laundry is piling up, dishes get dirty, students go back to school, etc. Life begins to return to normal, but what is normal now? I had always rested in the fact that "God won't give you more than you can handle." When others suffered tragic loss, pain and illness, I felt safe. After all, I couldn't handle that so it won't come. I was wrong! I can't find that phrase in the Bible. (I think we often take 1 Cor. 10:13 out of context, but that is referring to temptation which is different from suffering) Crushing, paralyzing, agonizing pain has come into my life. This is more than I can handle on my own. I can only handle this with God's help. That is the assurance I am resting on today. God is walking along beside us. I know without a doubt God is carrying us. I don't know what normal is now but I know whatever it is, God is beside me walking the path. If I can't take the next step, He is carrying me. "

September 28, 2020: " After Grant's service this past Saturday, I had decided to not post anything else on Facebook for a while. But God just keeps on speaking to me. Yesterday was tough for me. I was on kind of a spiritual high after Saturday. Then on Sunday, I started seeing "National Sons Day" posts. I debated on whether to post a picture of my three sons. However, I felt God telling me that even though Grant is now in heaven it doesn't change the fact that we still have 2 amazing sons and 1 amazing daughter here on earth with us. I love what our pastor Dr. McWhite said a few weeks ago in his sermon. If we know where something/someone is, are they really lost? We know where Grant is now so we haven't lost him. God has graciously provided for our family abundantly through our walk. He knows exactly what we need, exactly when we need it. He created us so therefore he knows our needs even before we do. We've been told of at least 3 salvations through these past few weeks. We've been told multiple times of parents being able to have open conversations with their teenagers about faith and life. We pray that these will continue to bring glory to our great God. I was reading this morning in a devotional about handling grief that someone had given us. It said, "Grief is a process. It is not an event. You can't avoid it. You can't rush it." In the days ahead, please pray for our family as we face constant reminders of Grant. We know this road will not be easy, but we know that God will carry us when we can't walk. His grace is sufficient.

I think that it is important to remember that when you lose a child, it is not just you that is affected. With so much attention being placed on Grant, sometimes I felt that I neglected my relationship with Kara, Callie, Jake and Zack. "National Son's Day" was a great reminder of my duty as leader of the house and our family to make sure that they were being taken care of as well. They were grieving as well.

September 30, 2020: "Not gonna lie. Yesterday was a tough day. I noticed that some of the flowers we have received have started wilting. Medical bills started arriving. Insurance claims had to be filed. Some of the "reality" of Grant's death crept back into our lives yesterday. We have found that grief is not a straight line. It's not a destination. It is often like a roller coaster which loops you back to emotions that you thought you had come to terms with. Why would God choose to take someone in their youth? Why wasn't Grant wearing a seatbelt? Questions that we asked in the very beginning of our journey. We knew these days would come. It doesn't make it any easier. We know the devil is not going to leave us alone. BUT, we also know that God is also not going to leave us alone. In our wrestling with emotions of anger and confusion yesterday, God kept sending us gentle reminders of his presence. We received a poster with all of the posts from his friends and teachers at WHHS. We were able to give Grant's basketball shoes to one of his closest friends and teammates. We certainly should not have been surprised. God has never failed us, and he never will. So as the visitors and cards slow down, we will continue to walk in God's peace. We know there will be other "yesterdays" in our future. We take comfort in the fact that the Lord will continue to "hold us fast".

Eventually, life continues on. The daily tasks of life start up again, whether you feel like you are ready are not. The number of visitors slows down. You are left with more time alone to ponder and think about your loss. You realize that time stops for no one. You can't hit pause or reset. To me, this was the hardest time. The time where I needed to rely on God even more.

October 1, 2020: "Caleb. Canyon. Emma. Grant. Matt. Clarence. Four 16 year old teenagers with so much hope and potential. One 31 year old firefighter who had just begun getting his life back in order. One 63 year old loving father and grandfather. All leaving this earth unexpectedly within just a few weeks of each other in our community. Why God? Why? Our earthly minds can't answer that question. We don't understand, but at the same time we do understand.....God says that this is just our temporary home. That life is like a vapor. A mist. A passing shadow. Jesus says in John 11:25, "I am the one who brings people back to life, and I am life itself. Those who believe in me will live even if they die. Everyone who lives and believes in me shall never die". I believe that Grant and the others are MORE alive now than they ever have been. We still have times of deep hurt. We still have days where we just want to lay on the couch and grieve. But God is good. He holds our hearts when they are breaking.

I'm reminded of a tapestry when thinking about life. The back looks so disjointed and random. Oftentimes it makes no sense. The front, however, looks so beautiful and perfect. Our life here on earth mirrors the back. Caleb, Canyon, Emma, Grant, Matt and Clarence can now see the front."

So much sorrow in the past few weeks. So many young lives taken from this earth. Parents and siblings left with giant holes in their family and hearts. The devil sure wants us to point a finger at and blame God. Our faith, even though sometimes shaken, is too strong to fall for his schemes.

October 2, 2020: "Up late tonight. Looking forward to attending Pickens High FCA in the morning. Continually amazed at God's presence and goodness. PHS has been SO good to me and my family through Grant's death. Such a special place. Go Blue Flame!

Once our kids started playing sports and driving, we got Life 360 on our phones. We could look (not snoop of course) and see where they were. Sense of security. We would always get a notification when they were either leaving home or were coming home. Again, security and peace of mind as a parent. The night of Sept 14, Grant had turned his app off. He was a typical 16 year old. Going to Cookout with his friends for a milkshake. We had already gone to bed. I'm sure he thought he would just slide back into bed when he got home. No harm. No foul. We never got that notification that Grant had arrived home.

If God has Life 360 (which of course he doesn't need) then on Sept 16 at 10:16 pm , He would've gotten a notification that Grant would've arrived home. Not to our earthly residence. But to his eternal home. In Heaven. With Him. Forever.

Oh, our soul feels so empty at times. Even after two weeks we still ask God the hard questions. But we serve a big and mighty God. There's nothing we can't bring to Him. Nothing overwhelms Him. When our strength ends, His begins.

There are many people in our community and circle of friends that are struggling with grief. Not just for Grant. So many other tragedies in the last few weeks. I pray that through all of them that we would point people to Jesus. He is good even when nothing in this world seems good. He has been our rock because without Him we could not lift our hands in praise. Worthy is He!"

I can't begin to adequately express the gratitude towards the students and staff at Pickens High School. From the very moment of learning of Grant's death to even today almost a year later, they have been a true blessing. The love I felt when I walked into the auditorium filled with students and teachers on Oct. 2 was overwhelming. It would continue in the months to come.

October 2, 2020: (Callie's words) "Right after Grant passed away I didn't want to post anything. It was too soon and hurt too much to even type anything out. I was awful at just responding to text messages. Then, I didn't have the words to say. However, over the past few days I have slowly typed out my thoughts.

I want to share a little bit about how I saw Grant. First, I called him Grantie 90% of the time. He is the only boy who has ever had a heart by his name in my contacts. If you are close to my family you probably know that it was Grant and me vs. Jake and Zack. I would go to bat for Grant way before I would for Jake or Zack. In terms of our family, Grant and I were a team. Whether it was Spikeball, sibling arguments, or literal fist fights I was always Team Grant. Grant made me laugh. He was goofy. My Snapchat memories are full of videos and pictures of him doing dumb things. However, he also drove me crazy. One time he used the blender to make a slushie at 1:00am and I almost lost my mind. He was also grumpy and sarcastic, we called him Grumpy Grant for a reason. I loved to poke fun at him because he could take it and would dish it right back out. I could write a whole book full of Grant stories and memories. I'll miss that red hair (even though I hated his long hair) every single day.

I am the saddest when I think about the hole in our family. Every year at the beach I would force my family to take a human pyramid picture. They hated it, but I kept nagging until they finally gave in. Our family is no longer a perfect pyramid. The only reason our pyramid is not crashing to the ground is because our foundation is in the Lord and His arms are wrapped so tightly around us. I am standing on the fact that His ways are higher than ours. God's plan is perfect even when it might seem like life is the opposite of perfect."

As a father, reading my daughter's words about her brother, my heart aches. It makes me realize that losing Grant affected a lot of people in many different ways. Not just me. There is not just one way to grieve. And I had to learn to allow people the space and time to deal with this loss. I had to learn that I could not just shut down. I had to provide comfort and love to others even in the middle of my own sorrow. That's what fathers should do.

October 3, 2020: Tough day today. Not sure why. Just woke up so sad. Knew these days would creep back in. So thankful we can lean on God.

Many days when we awake, we are unaware of what that day holds in store for us. We hope and pray that it's a good day. Oftentimes that is the case. But then there are those days where you wish you could just crawl back in bed or even go back in time to change things in our life. Not every day is spent on the top of the mountain. Sometimes we must experience the valleys in life so that we will appreciate the mountain tops. I have often gone back in my mind to think of anything that I could've done differently leading up to Grant's accident that somehow would've changed the outcome. I have learned that God set a plan for Grant's life far before he entered this earth. He knew this day would come. We can't beat ourselves up over the choices or decisions that others make. Our job is to just trust that God knows what He is doing.

At this point, I knew I was going back to work. I knew that at some point I had to. I wasn't sure if I was emotionally ready. The students and faculty of Pickens High School let me know really quickly that they were going to support me in love and prayer. What a special place to work!

Back to Reality

October 5, 2020: First day back at work since Sept. 14. Loved seeing all of my students. Multiple staff members came by and checked on me today. It meant a lot to me. BUT today was VERY hard. I'll be honest. Teaching quadratic equations was not on the top of my mind this morning. I struggled all weekend how to walk back into class and resume "normal". What should I say? Do I ignore all that has happened in my life the past few weeks? How do I use Grant's death as a way to witness not only to my students but colleagues as well? Obviously, I am limited by law on how much I can share with my students. I tried to speak freely about my emotional status. I pray my spiritual status shone through as well.

As the shock and numbness wears off, reality starts to become more apparent. Less visitors, less cards, hospital bills, insurance issues, going back to work. We knew these days would come. We still miss Grant just as much but then have to deal with all of this other stuff as well.

I was inspired so much by Lorry Houston Burkins last night. She was interviewed during our Night of Worship at church last evening. She is battling Stage 4 breast cancer. She is such a beast and such an encouragement to us! She made the comment that so many people keep telling her how strong she is. Her response was that she is so weak and that God is providing strength. How honest and true. Kara and I have felt some of the same strength through dealing with Grant's death. But it is not our own. His strength is perfect when our strength is gone.

Lorry would pass away just a few months later. Her spirit never dimmed. Our life group class at church surrounded her and her family with prayer. She fought to the very end with such grace and composure. But God called her home just as he did Grant. Our family grew in strength as we watched her and her husband Robert show such strength. Her spirit here on earth lives on just as we know Grant's does as well.

October 6, 2020: This year started my 26th year of coaching high school basketball. I've been at multiple schools at various positions. From C- team to Varsity. From assistant to head coach. I honestly have struggled the past few weeks on whether I had it in me to continue. Grant LOVED basketball. He loved playing it. He loved watching it. He loved talking about it with me. I was afraid there would be too many reminders this upcoming season of Grant for me to totally invest in this season.

All along our journey through Grant's death I have constantly talked about God showing His presence to us just when we needed it. I came to Pickens HS last year. I could tell very quickly how special a place it was. Not to diminish the other schools that I've been at. I've been blessed at every coaching stop in many different ways with tremendous players and people.

Some of the first texts/messages I received after Grant passed away were from my players at Pickens. I love each of them dearly and I felt their love for me as well. I know it's not easy for teenage boys to share their emotions. But these guys just reached out to me honestly. It made my decision to coach this year an easy one. We had our first conditioning "practice" this afternoon since last season. I wasn't sure what to say or do. I've done this forever. Why would I struggle with this? I quickly realized the family that we have created in just a year. We just picked up where we had left off. I love these boys as if they were my own. Grant would've fit right in with these guys. He was such a special young man and so are these guys that I have the honor to coach this year. Go Blue Flame! "For I know the plans I have for you, declares the Lord. Plans to prosper you and not to harm you, plans to give you hope and a future." Jeremiah 29:11

I really don't know if I could've been able to coach again if it were not for this special group of young men at Pickens High School. Austin Hall, my point guard, asked me if he could change his number to #0 in honor of Grant. Wow. What a special group of young men. I know I continue to say it, but God knows what you need when you need it. I needed these boys.

This group of young men would go on to break a 57 game losing streak that year. More importantly though, they were there for me when I needed them the most.

October 7, 2020: "Sacrifice. That is what my devotion was about this morning. I would like to think that in my past I would be willing to sacrifice for God. Not a goat or ram as was once done. But something of value to me. My currency.

While in the hospital with Grant, I kept asking God, oftentimes audibly, for God to take me instead of him. I offered to take his place if God would just choose to spare him. I would trade my 48 years on this earth for his 16. I looked forward to seeing what God had in store for his life. That wasn't God's plan. Looking back, I ask myself,"Who am I to tell God what He needs to do?" I'm not God. But He is.

We so often are caught up in what God's plan is for our life. It really is quite simple. Obedience. His will is not tied to a job, a spouse, a location, a family....just obedience. Obedience when life pumps us up. Obedience when life knocks us to our knees. Obedience when God gives. Obedience when God chooses to take your 16 year old son. Obedience in the sunshine. Obedience in the storms. Seems simple doesn't it? If it were so simple then God would not have had to sacrifice His only Son so that we might experience hope and life eternal. Oftentimes it is hard for us. We don't understand. Why does God answer some prayers so quickly? Why does God answer some prayers with a no or a not yet? Only good comes from God. There's no way we can wrap our human brain around how God answers our prayers. We just have to trust that He does. Not my will but thine will. There will come a day when we will have full understanding. Grant knows now. One day we will too."

October 9, 2020: "Every morning when I get to school, I have a choice to make. Do I want to see today or do I want to wear a mask? Because if you wear glasses like me you know that doing both is nearly impossible. And keeping my glasses clean is another futile task. I'm constantly cleaning them. Or looking for that little cloth to clean them with. 2020 has been something else.

I started thinking about vision. Through what lens of life do we look through? The world offers its lens but it's like wearing a mask and glasses. Foggy. Cloudy. Uncertain. Hopeless. Then there is the lens that Jesus offers. Clear. Certain. Hopeful. Perfect.

I've tried both sets of lenses in dealing with Grant's death. The lens of the world...why would God choose to take the life of such a young man with so much life ahead of him? Why me? How is my family supposed to move forward? The lens of Jesus....Jeff, I've got this. You don't understand right now but trust me. I've never failed you and I'm not about to start now. When you can't seem to move forward, I will carry you.

*The writer of Hebrews says, "**Fix your eyes on Jesus**". That means our focus needs to be vertical. Our relationship with Him should guide us, not the world and the circumstances it throws at us. Too often our focus is horizontal, completely allowing our circumstances to dictate our lives, our reactions, our behaviors. The world wants our focus. And let's be honest. We constantly allow it to change our lens. It steals our joy. It questions our faith. It causes division. We all know this and have experienced this. But somehow we keep changing glasses.*

Grant now sees clearly. Perfect vision. I can hear him right now looking down at me and saying, "Dad, why are you worrying about this or that? Why are you letting the world get you down? God's in charge, not the world." On the days where I feel deep pain for the loss of my son, I'm sure he's saying to me, "Just be patient, dad. You're going to love this place. All of that junk down there is no longer. I'll see you soon. Take good care of mom, Callie, Jake and Zack." One day, I will no longer have to choose glasses or a mask. Covid will be forgotten. 2020 will only be a blip. Death and pain will be no more. I will finally get to truly see. Just as Grant does."

Thankfully some of the Covid protocols were lifted and mask mandates were ended in the months to come. My glasses were no longer foggy all of the time.

October 10, 2020: "That day when evening came, he said to his disciples, "Let us go over to the other side." Leaving the crowd behind, they took him along, just as he was, in the boat. There were also other boats with him. A furious squall came up, and the waves broke over the boat, so that it was nearly swamped. Jesus was in the stern, sleeping on a cushion. The disciples woke him and said to him, "Teacher, don't you care if we drown?" He got up, rebuked the wind and said to the waves, "Quiet! Be still!" Then the wind died down and it was completely calm. He said to his disciples, "Why are you so afraid? Do you still have no faith?" They were terrified and asked each other, "Who is this? Even the wind and waves obey him!" Mark 4:35-41

The forecast for this weekend calls for rain. Your reaction to that really depends on your perspective. If you just planted grass seed, then you're probably pretty excited. If you were planning on attending a football game or picnic today, then probably not so much. The threat of rain can either dampen your spirits or give you some hope. Part of today calls for 100% rain. Those are pretty high odds. Probably going to happen.

In our lives we pretty much live with a 100% chance of rain. God promises us that there will be rain/trials in our life. Knowing Him does not shield us from pain and loss. We went to bed on September 14 thinking that the next day we would wake up and do what we normally do on a typical morning. However, the rain came quickly to our family on September 15. He does, however, provide us protection and hope when the rains do come just as he did with his disciples in the boat. He'll never give us too much rain. That he promises. We might have struggled early on believing that. Like the disciples, we felt as if we might drown. But looking back now, we know he was always right there with us.

The absence of rain causes drought. Which leads to death. It robs us of opportunities for growth. How do you praise the rain when it comes into your life? How do you count it as joy? How do you lift your heart and hands to God when your 16 year old son is taken from this earth? Certainly not from our own strength or power. It only comes from His perfect strength and amazing grace. It is the only way that we can grow.

Rain reminds me of a baseball trip the "boys" took back in 2015. Kara's dad, Jake , Grant, Parker and I were in Pittsburgh. Our hotel was about half a mile to a mile away from downtown. We decided one afternoon to walk downtown just to get some lunch and check out the city. It seemed like right when we got downtown that it started to rain. We had no umbrellas. It was in July so it was still pretty warm even in Pittsburgh. At first we were all a little bummed that we were getting wet. At some point I guess we just embraced it and enjoyed it. The rain wasn't going to hurt us. We knew the rain would eventually stop and the sun would appear. We basically decided to dance (not literally haha) in the rain. I guess you could say we counted it as joy that day.

When it starts to rain in your life, what is your response? I'm a firm believer in God's promises. One of his promises is symbolized by a rainbow. I don't normally quote Dolly

Parton, but she said once, *"you can't have a rainbow without a little rain."* You know what happens after you see a rainbow? The sun starts shining again. We don't see Grant's death as an end but as a beginning. Find a reason to dance in the rain today. Soon enough, you will see the sun. Our God promises. And He keeps His promises. You can put 100% on that as well. For eternity."

I would use this post as the foundation of my message to FCA's at Pickens High School, Travelers Rest High School and Wade Hampton High School in future weeks to come.

October 11, 2020: Today was the first Sunday both Kara and I were back at church together. It was also the first Sunday for me back in the choir. It felt good. It felt right. Something normal. Our college minister spoke out of Psalms 34. We even sang Psalm 34 by Brooklyn Tabernacle Choir in the choir. When we were in the hospital with Grant, I started making a playlist (if you have Spotify, look up Fly High Grant) of songs that were meaningful to me. Music has been one of my greatest comforts through our journey of grief. One of the first songs I added was "Psalms 34". I was worried that I might get emotional in the choir loft this morning as we sang it but I held it together. Grant would've told me to stop being soft, but that's okay.

Today was also baby dedication Sunday. It's always neat and refreshing to see young parents bring their children before God and promise to teach and lead them in God's ways. We've had the privilege to do this four times at TFBC with our children. I don't think we ever looked that young, but maybe we did. It saddens us that we will not get to see Grant's children dedicated. I thought of Grant this morning sitting in church, as three of the babies being dedicated had red hair. Even our college minister has red hair. Something about red hair. I looked up at the pew at the very top of the balcony where he and his friends always sat. He wasn't there physically, but he was there. We miss that red hair.

Births and baby dedications are exciting events. The newness of life. The hope of a future. A new beginning. As adults we are often like those newborns. Unsure of life. Unsure of our future. Helpless. Hopeless. Each day gives a new opportunity, however, to determine the direction of our lives. Whatever your Monday morning involves...school, home, job, etc. , WE get to CHOOSE how our day or week goes. No matter how yesterday or last week ended, tomorrow can be different. One of my favorite songs says, "When I'm standing on the mountain, I didn't get there on my own. When I'm walking through the valley, I know I am not alone". There are two things we choose to be each day no matter if it is on the mountain or in the valley. You're either a joy giver or a joy stealer. You can either provide hope or you can provide harm. You may be someone's answered prayer who desperately needs joy and hope in their life. But you also might be too wrapped up in your own world to even notice your hurting co-worker or neighbor.

There is no greater joy than the joy of serving others.

Our enemy desires chaos over calm. He desires guilt over grace. Which do you choose?. I choose Him. Whatever mistakes I made yesterday or last week or even years ago, I lay at the feet of Jesus. He gives me a fresh start. Each and every day. He makes beauty from ashes. I challenge you, including myself, to live your faith out loud this week instead of on mute. Serve Him by serving others.

I wonder if Grant's kids would've inherited that long red "flow"? I would like to think so."

October 12, 2020: From the day Kara and I met in 1995, she was always on me about going to see the dermatologist. Not nagging (maybe a little, love you dear). I fought it for many years. I'm a man. I'll be fine. I don't need to stop for directions. Lol. After 18 years of "gentle" reminders, I decided to take her advice. In 2014, the doctor took a sample of an irregular mole that was on my left cheek on my face. A few days later, we got a call. Melanoma. Cancer. I was pretty devastated. In my mind, I was still too young to deal with the "c" word. I had surgery not too much longer after that. Praise God they were able to remove it all. When I took the bandage off in front of Zack, who was only four years old at the time, his response was "Seven!". My scar looks just like the number seven. If you haven't noticed it before, I'll ignore the fact that you are staring at my face the next time I see you. Haha. It is part of my "story". It is a permanent reminder of a trial in my life that was tough but that God led me through. I am constantly asked about my scar.

Scars. Sometimes they are physical but many times they are below the surface. Emotional scars. Spiritual scars. Grant arrived at the hospital on Sept. 15 with some devastating injuries. Injuries that he would never recover from. On Sept. 16, when he entered heaven, all of his wounds and past scars were removed. He was made perfect. He experienced the same thing that our Lord did when he arrived at his heavenly home with God after the cross. How amazing is that? The most famous wounds in history, in our savior's hands and feet, disappeared immediately in the presence of God. Just as Grant's did. Wow!

We all have scars. From that time you fell off your bike. That time you had surgery. That time you did something you probably should not have been doing. Hey guys, watch this. All of those are visible. What about the time you said something hurtful to a loved one? What about divorce? What about that time you fell away from or even lost faith in God? In our case, what about that time you learned your son was leaving this world? Though not visible, hidden scars are just as painful.

Often we try to hide our physical scars and bury our emotional or spiritual scars. They are often jagged or ugly. They bring up deep pain that often we just want to suppress and leave alone. My "seven" on my face is kind of hard to hide, but having to wear a mask has helped (even though I would much rather show my scar). But a lot of times our scars, both visible and invisible to the human eye, are our stories. They are opportunities for us to have conversations. How'd you get that scar? Conversations lead us to sharing our faith with people. God can work with the deepest, most painful scar. He can certainly relate. If you think you're the only one who's ever gone through what you have been through or are currently going through, you're mistaken. We have had several people who have lost children reach out to us that before this happened were complete strangers. They shared their story with us. They gave us hope. We realized that we are not alone. Your story may need to be heard by someone else. I went back to a post from the other day. Obedience. Even when it is not comfortable. Lost people will never come to know Jesus without conversations. Maybe it's time to uncover your scars and share your story. Someone needs to hear it. The "seven" on my face? One day it will be erased. That's hope. That's what this world needs to hear. Thank you God for our scars. May we use them to tell our story and lead people to You."

October 13, 2020: And God said, "Let there be light," and there was light. God saw that the light was good, and he separated the light from the darkness. Genesis 1:3-4

When was the last time you were in complete darkness? Probably during a power outage. I don't know of many people who willingly choose to live in complete darkness. What do people do during a power outage? They look for light. Find that flashlight. Shoot, the batteries are dead. Find that old oil lamp. Man, out of oil. What are we thinking? We can just use the flashlight on our fancy phone. Sheesh, only 3% left.

The power went out in our house several nights ago. We always worry when there is a storm with heavy rain and high winds that we might lose power. You kind of wait in nervous anticipation that at any moment it will go dark. Those several flickers. Oh no. Just wait. It's coming. But the other night, it was completely calm. Totally unexpected. Ends up that a transformer blew in our neighborhood. Regardless of the reason, pitch black. That sudden moment of despair and helplessness.

I was up listening to music in my recliner with my headphones in when it went dark. No warning whatsoever. I thought the girls had just turned the lights out on me before going to bed. I even tried to turn on the lamp next to me. Nothing. We've all been there. Trying to turn on the light switch when obviously there will be no result. Kara found a flashlight. That added a little light. Enough to function. We started finding more alternative sources of light. The house got a little brighter with each device. We began to feel a little more safe and secure. Then it happened (thankfully after a really short time). The house came to life. The alarm clocks started flashing. Full light and power again. Is that not the most satisfying thing when you've been without power? You feel like it's the brightest your house has ever been. Almost blinding.

One of the comments we heard a lot from Grant's friends was how he could "light up a room". I can imagine it came naturally to him. When you're 6'3" with long flowing red hair and a witty personality, sometimes on the side of smart-alecky (not sure if that's a word), it is hard to hide. Physically, he didn't really blend in.

I have really tried to examine my own life to make sure that I don't just blend in. You and I have something that a lot of this world does not have, but desperately needs. Light. There's a reason people get up early to go see a magnificent sunrise or sit on the beach late in the afternoon to see a glorious sunset. There's a reason we put night lights in our bedrooms. There's a reason we put motion detector lights outside our homes. Light brings security. Light brings hope. Light is life. The world needs light. The world needs life. The light and life that only Jesus can provide. They are searching for light, even though they may not admit it. We all search for it. If you know Jesus, then you've found it. But just because you have found light in your life doesn't mean that the lights can't go off unexpectedly. Ours did the night of Sept.15. We are slowly trying to find that light again. We have assurance it will come back on.

Do we brighten up a room or a relationship when we walk in? Or do we just blend in. It's so easy to blend in. Just blending in is like being a flashlight with no batteries or a phone with no charge. Useless. With each light we shine, the world becomes a little brighter. It takes all of our lights. But God is that ultimate light. That feeling when the power comes back on in your house. That feeling when a lost person experiences the amazing moment when they go from complete darkness to glorious, life changing light. God looked at the light and said it was good. It must be good if He thinks so. Because only good comes from Him. Let your light shine today."

October 13, 2020:" Vocabulary.com defines blessed as lucky to have something. I'm sorry. Our family being blessed has nothing to do with luck. Our God doesn't deal in luck. He deals in truth. And hope . Kara's college friends bought her the basket to put all of the cards we have received during Grant's death. We truly appreciate such a sweet gesture. But we need a bigger box. Lol. Overwhelmed doesn't even come close to what we have felt from the love of family and friends. We have felt guilt for not being there for our friends and family like people have been there for us. A HUGE wake up call. God has been tremendous for us. An anchor. I pray that we could help share that hope and security for others. I pray that you could provide that for someone else. Now's not the time to be silent. It's time to share the victory that we put our hope in. Time to be loud. And Proud."

October 14, 2020: "Have you ever dropped a plate or a glass onto the floor? Even one of those fluorescent bulbs in your garage. They just shatter. Pieces go everywhere. You try your best to sweep up all of the pieces but it is almost impossible to get every tiny one. Unfortunately, you normally find one in the middle of the night, days later when you're not wearing shoes or socks. They hurt and often cause you to bleed.

Our family was shattered on a very early Tuesday morning in September. We were awakened to the news of Grant's accident. News that we neither expected nor were prepared for. Shattered. Our once "whole" family was in pieces right before us. As the days have passed, we've had good days and not so good days, mostly good though. Days where we felt like we were starting to get back on our feet. But then we come across one of those tiny hidden pieces that reopens a wound or cuts us in a fresh way. How do you deal with those tiny pieces?

We believe that God is a god of restoration. Our family will never be the "whole" that it was before Sept. 16. He has given us a new "whole". He has taken the pieces of our broken family and put them back together again. One piece at a time. One moment at a time. He's not done with us. There will still be days down the road where we will find more shards of glass. And they'll hurt. And we might bleed. And we'll shed tears. And yet we will continue to praise Him. We don't have to stay shattered. He will restore us. Praise God."

October 14, 2020: "The past 36 hours have felt like one of those roller coaster rides of grief that people talk about. I've talked about Life 360 in previous posts. I always check to see if Kara has made it to work, or if Callie has made it back to Clemson, or if Jake has moved at all during the day (just kidding Jake). At the bottom of our family page has always been "Bucket Getter". That was Grant. His self-proclaimed Life 360 nickname. Since Sept. 14, it has said "services have been turned off." For a while, I didn't pay much attention to it but it continued to just remind me of the whole night of the accident. I talked with Kara and we both decided it was probably time to take him off of our family page. Sounds easy? So tough. Something so small as a simple press of a settings button on a phone. Something so significant though to us. Has it really been a month since the night of his accident? Some days it seems like yesterday. Other days it seems like an eternity ago. We have loved getting reminders of Grant through this whole journey. We have cried, smiled, laughed (a lot!) and remembered him in such special ways. Something about taking him off of that Life 360 family page just hit so hard though. Seemed so permanent. The bottom of the roller coaster.*

HOWEVER, roller coasters always rise again. I have been praying on a prayer request in my professional life for the last nine months. It was answered today. In an amazing way. No details right now but trust me. Nothing but God. One of Grant's closest friends, Hayden, came over this afternoon to our house. He just came to hang out. He shot basketball, played video games and just spent time with Zack. He ended up staying and eating supper with us. After supper, we just sat on the couch and told Grant stories. Pretty impressive thing for a teenage boy. Just another reminder of God's goodness. Nothing planned or expected. But I really think that is when God does His best work. When we least expect it. When we need it the most. I love what our sweet friend Lorry Burkins, who is battling cancer, said in her interview with Fox the other night. "I've had good days and bad days. But they're all God days." Amen, Lorry. May we see every day as a God day. If you're at the bottom of the roller coaster right now, just wait. You're going to rise again. And it will be amazing. He is the God of all of our days."

October 16, 2020: "My journey through grief really started with these 3 words. Urgent prayer needed. Today is the one month anniversary of Grant's death. Little did I know what those 3 words would evolve into. At the time I posted, there were so many unknowns. Looking back, there are still some unknowns. But there are also some "knowns". Our family is extremely blessed with amazing support from our friends, church, community and even complete strangers. Our God is incredible. He has allowed us to come to Him with all of our emotions, even the ugly ones. Grant gets to spend eternity with our Savior and we will be reunited with him down the road. Our faith will be turned to sight. Those are "knowns" that have increased our faith and brought our family closer together and closer to Him.

To see or hear my musical playlist is like walking through our journey of grief. I hit shuffle and I can vividly remember when each song ministered to me. The night of the accident, the anxious waiting in the hospital, that last test that did not give us the answer we wanted, the process of organ donation, writing Grant's obituary, planning his funeral, going back to work and all the days since. My new phrase from Lorry Burkins is "all days are God days." I know my playlist is not finished because I know God is not finished. What He started, He will see to completion. Just as Grant's story continues, so does mine.

I keep telling people that I really am not a writer. Dr. Cliff and his yellow bound notes (if you're my age, you'll get that) got me through high school English. Sorry Mrs. Bridges. You were really cool. Silas Marner not so much. God has just spoken such truth to me that I felt honored to write it down and share. It has helped me cope and heal. When I feel like I am running out of words, God keeps supplying. I've been overwhelmed with the number of people who have read, shared and commented on my posts. I pray that God has shone through every post. I may have typed the words, but they were His.

Basketball season begins in two weeks. My busy season. What I feel is my true ministry. With that being said, I think I'm going to take a little bit of a break. A time for more inward, private reflection. God may change my plans. If he does then there will be more "Just a minute with Jeff"'s. Hopefully some good news from Pickens basketball as well. Lol. Please continue to pray for the Harrelsons. Please pray for me as basketball starts that I would lead these young men in a way that is pleasing to God."

October 17, 2020:" God is amazing. One of the amazing things about God is that he often uses other people in our lives to speak to us. Or He even brings complete strangers into our lives to do the same. Before going to bed last night, I received a message from one of those strangers. After reading her message, I realized we weren't really strangers. Even though we have never met, we share a common experience of loss . God has led us both through all of the pain and darkness. I don't know what led Lori to reaching out to me late last night. Well, actually I do. God.

I was going to take a break from posting until getting that message last night. If God asks you to do something, then you do it. You don't think about it. You don't try to justify it. You just do it. I started doing some math (that's what I do) and realized that there are 50 days until Grant's birthday. There are also a little over 50 songs on my Grant playlist. A few of those songs I have already posted, but that's okay. I decided to call this idea "Days of Praise". Hopefully just a reminder to find joy in every circumstance. On the good days. On the bad days. The God days. A quick verse, a quick song and a quick thought."

Days of Praise

Days of Praise: Day #1

"The Lord is my shepherd, I lack nothing. He makes me lie down in green pastures, he leads me beside quiet waters, he refreshes my soul. He guides me along the right paths for his name's sake." Psalm 23:1-3

It's Gameday. Grant's favorite. The anticipation. The buildup. The hype. Covid has put a little bit of a damper on our traditional festivities. Virtual tailgating just doesn't quite have the same feel does it? I pray that no matter what the scoreboard says at the end of the game for your favorite team, that you will choose joy today. Take a moment to "lie down". Find the "quiet waters" somewhere today. He deserves all of our praise. As He says, we lack nothing. So as we yell out today, "Go Tigers, or Seminoles, or Gamecocks". Don't forget a huge "Go God".

Days of Praise: Day #2
"I will praise you, O Lord my God, with all of my heart, and I will glorify your name forevermore." Psalm 86:12

In a few short hours we will walk into a sanctuary. What are your expectations? Do you even feel like going? How often do we drag our baggage in with us? We often focus on what we will get out of the service. But that is not what worship is about. It is what WE can offer GOD. HE deserves our worship. HE deserves our praise. Let's leave our baggage at the door and give Him the honor He deserves. It's not about us. It is about HIM. He has given us so much and asks so little in return. Let's give Him today what he truly deserves. Our full attention and worship. May He be praised today.

Days of Praise: Day #3
"Even though I walk through the valley of the shadow of death, I will fear no evil, for you are with me, your rod and your staff, they comfort me." Psalm 23:4

Fear. It can be crippling. Paralyzing. What are your fears? What are you afraid of? My fears are heights and snakes. I used to love roller coasters. No more. I prefer my feet on the ground. As far as snakes go, my philosophy is that the only good snake is a dead snake. Grant didn't really have any fears (how many 16 year old boys do?). Except maybe books and reading. Lol. Maybe you fear change. Or commitment. Or the dark. Maybe it is Monday mornings. No matter what it is, control what you can control. You can control your attitude. Your words. Your smile. Your witness. One of the opposites of fear is love. Let tomorrow morning be the best Monday morning ever. Show your world a love that can only be explained by Jesus. He overcame the world. We have nothing to fear. There's not one thing that this world can throw at us that we cannot claim victory over. The same power that Jesus showed the world on the cross and through His resurrection is the same power that He has provided for us here on earth through His Holy Spirit. Instead of seeing tomorrow morning as an obligation, see it as an opportunity. An opportunity to show His mercy and goodness. Be the light in someone's darkness. That you can control.

Days of Praise: Day #4

"God is our refuge and strength, an ever present help in trouble. Therefore, we will not fear, though the earth gives way and the mountains fall into the sea." Psalm 46:1-2

Ever been heartbroken? Of course you have. Ever felt like the rug has just been pulled out from under you? Or blindsided? I know I have. You may be at that stage in your life right now. We all have experienced pain and loss in our lives. It often comes unexpected which makes it that more difficult. Our family knows that we will never fully be healed on earth from Grant's death, but we are trying to heal a little each day. Healing doesn't happen in a moment. Or a day. Or a week. Or sometimes even years. Only in His presence will we be fully healed. What do you do when you feel like you have hit rock bottom? You get on your knees and lift your arms and praise God. Even when it's the last thing you feel like doing. Even if you are asking Him why. Even if you are angry with Him. God didn't cause or plan Grant's accident. I fully believe that. But when we learned he had taken his last breath, the last thing I felt like doing was praising Him. But I did it. How? Because His strength begins at the bottom of our rope. Why? Because He says, "It's going to be okay." And I have no reason to doubt Him.

Days of Praise: Day #5

"And going a little farther he fell on his face and prayed,"My Father, if it be possible, let this cup pass from me; nevertheless, not my will, but thy will."" Matthew 26:39

It is well with my soul. If you grew up in a baptist church, you probably remember this old hymn. Easy to say if everything is going your way. Not so much if you're in a dark place or going through the fire. Grant's death has taught me a lot about prayer. It has taught me that prior to his accident, my prayer life was not what it needed to be. It was like a vending machine. I would only go to God in prayer if I needed something. I would hear prayer requests and kind of store them in my mind, usually forgetting about them some time later. I have committed myself now, if at all possible, to when I hear a request to stop what I am doing and pray right then. I now praise him every morning. The other thing it has taught me is how God answers prayers. We prayed really hard for a miracle. We knew He was able and we knew that He could in spite of what science and medicine said. We didn't get what we asked for. I will be honest. We felt a little abandoned at the time. Why would God not spare Grant? SO MANY people were on their knees with us. But God had other plans. He provided miracles to four people through Grant's organs. If He had granted Jesus' request to take the cup from Him, we would not have received forgiveness of sins through the cross. I pray that EVEN IF God does not grant us our wishes in prayer, or we come to a dark place in our life, or He chooses to leave mountains unmovable we can say "It is well with my soul."

Little did I know that after I wrote this , we would receive one of the best letters ever. We found out the age and gender of the recipients of Grants four organs that were donated. Thank you God for miracles. It is definitely well with my soul.

October 20, 2020: *"The letter we've been waiting for. God is amazing.*
Grant's heart: 62 year old male in Carolinas.
Grant's left kidney: 62 year old male in Carolinas
Grant's right kidney: 35 year old female in Carolinas
Grant's liver: 66 year old female in Midwest.

God definitely answers prayer. "

Days of Praise: Day #6
"I press on towards the goal for the prize of the upward call of God in Christ Jesus."
Philippians 3:14

Hindsight is always 20/20. It is so easy to look back at our lives and see our mistakes. We do it all the time. If I'd just done this or that. Or I certainly regret doing that. What was I thinking? Or to realize that God was walking with us not only through our tough times but our happy times as well. It's okay to look back and remember Grant. We will forever do that. There are reminders almost every day of him. Getting the letter yesterday about his organ donations was such a blessing. And an answered prayer for a miracle. Not ours but someone else's. We hope to one day meet the recipients. Where do we go from here though? There's a reason that the rear view mirror in our car is much smaller than the windshield. We need to be able to look back from time to time but we really need to focus on what is ahead of us. We will continue to honor Grant's memory by honoring our God. We will use every opportunity to share Grant's story. We pray that it will bring glory to God. We pray that it will bring people to God. We will praise Him through all of it because we have felt Him through all of it. Wins or losses. Happiness or tears. Sunshine or rain.

Days of Praise: Day #7
"You have turned for me my mourning into dancing." Psalm 30:11

Grace. Unmerited mercy or favor that God has given us through His son Jesus Christ. Grace truly is amazing as we so often sing. It is the greatest gift that a person can ever receive. We should celebrate it daily, not hide it or keep it to ourselves. As the song below says, the second you realize what's inside this gift, there's a few things that should happen.

Sing. I can do that thanks to Kathy Cochran, Pam Mayfield and Jane Hardin (my music teachers in elementary, middle and high school). Glide. Not sure my 48 year old body can really glide but I'll give it a try. Laugh. That one's easy. Smile. I need to do this more. Dance. This is definitely not a talent of mine. Nor Grant's.

God's grace should cause a joy in us that spills over. It should be evident to the world. Uncontrollable. When I get in a funk though, I tend to do the opposite. Sulk. Slouch. Groan. Scowl. Complain. Why in the world would anybody who does not know God want to be a part of that? We are called to be different. Different in the way we act and talk. Not just blending in. Hopeful. Joyful. Loving. Magnetic. That's what the world needs to see and hear from us.

October 23, 2020: *"Gorgeous sunrise at Pickens HS this morning. I had the privilege of speaking at FCA this morning and it was really special to me that my dad was able to come support me. I'm pretty sure Grant was looking down this morning. Another one of those God moments."*

Days of Praise: Day #8
"To bestow on them a crown of beauty instead of ashes, the oil of joy instead of mourning, and a garment of praise instead of a spirit of despair." Isaiah 61:3

One of Kara's favorite shows is the Hart of Dixie. Not at the top of my list but to each his or her own. I made the comment to her the other day that all of the people on that show look like movie stars (I guess in a way they are). Perfectly made up. Flawless almost. Can't be real life. Where are the people who look like me? They don't seem to make it onto the camera for some reason.

None of us are physically flawless. We all have bumps, bruises and scars. But everyone on this earth has the opportunity to become spiritually flawless. The cross gives us that opportunity. The millionaire CEO. The stay at home mom. The homeless person on the corner. The prisoner. The 16 year old red headed teenager. We are all made in the image of God. God desires for all of us to come to know Him. There is NO one that is TOO lost that He would not seek after. We make judgments about people all the time based on their appearance. What if God judged us the way we judge others? None of us would be worthy. That's the beauty of the cross. It doesn't discriminate. It makes beauty out of ashes. To ALL who seek Him.

Days of Praise: Day #9

"For I am the Lord your God who takes hold of your right hand and says to you, Do not fear; I will help you." Isaiah 41:13

Small reminders. Just the simplest and smallest things. Looking up to the balcony in the church where Grant used to sit. Looking over at the couch where we used to watch college football together. Listening to the quiet when there used to be a buzz of activity down stairs with his friends. Kara and I have both tried to show strength to Callie, Jake and Zack. But there are times where we have just had to sit down in our sadness. The need to just be held. Not forever but just for a moment. God has been there for us in those moments. The support from our family, friends, church and community have truly been an anchor for us as well. We have not one time felt inconvenienced, burdened or bothered by any visit, call, message or card. They have given us energy and encouragement. So when you don't know whether you should come by or not...come. When you don't know whether or not you should call...call. When you don't know the words to say...simply pray and still come. When you don't know if you should reach out...reach out. Your presence could be just the help that we need at that moment. You may be an answered prayer.

Days of Praise: Day #10

"And my God will supply every need of yours according to His riches in glory in Christ Jesus." Philippians 4:19

We used to try and convince Grant how good he had it. Back in our day, if you needed to know something, you had to slog through grandma's set of Encyclopedia Britannicas. Or in college, spending hours in the basement of a musty, poorly lit library looking at microfiche. Remember waiting on the Sears catalog to come in the mail so you could pick out what you wanted for Christmas? Or getting a busy signal and having to redial on that old rotary

phone? Ugh. No Google. No Amazon. No smart phones. Of course, we didn't know any
better at the time. These days you can have anything you want in an instant at the click of a
button or the swipe of a screen. All about convenience.

The song "Untitled Hymn" by Chris Rice was sung at Grant's celebration service. It's one of
my favorite songs. I have often wondered about the title, or lack of one. It really speaks of
all of the ways we can approach or experience Jesus. Maybe the songwriter didn't want to
just emphasize one of them. All just as important. Hurting? Come to Him. Saved? Sing to
Him. Fallen down? Fall on Him. Lonely? Cry to Him. Full of joy? Dance to Him. And then
the line that means the most to me as I am reminded of Grant: "And with your final
heartbeat, kiss the world goodbye. Then go in peace and laugh on glory's side. Fly to Jesus
and live." Oh what that must feel like. If I had to title the song it would be "Grant's Hymn".
Jesus has been everything for our family. No click of a button or special app necessary.
Whatever we have needed. At the exact moment we needed it. The only convenience that
truly matters or makes a difference. Keep flying high Grant.

Days of Praise: Day #11
"Then Moses stretched out his hand over the sea and the Lord drove the sea back by a
strong east wind all night and made the sea dry land and the waters were divided."
Exodus 14:21

Most people really love the beach or really hate it. We are definitely beach lovers. We have
enjoyed many years of going to the beach with our family. Hilton Head for spring break.
Folly Beach for summer vacation. Some of our best family memories are from the beach.
Callie making dribble castles. Jake skimboarding in the surf. Grant spending hours putting
into a man made golf hole in the sand. Zack boogie boarding in the waves. I remember
when each of our kids were little, how we would shield them from the ocean. We would
watch them like hawks on the beach. We would hold their hands to make sure they didn't
get knocked over by an incoming wave. Or as they got a little older, we would hold both
hands and help them jump the waves. Even as our children have grown, we still worry at
times when they get too far out. I think the ocean is so terrifying sometimes because of the
unknown.

Our life often is like the Israelites in the passage from Exodus above. You feel the enemy
bearing down on you. Your only path forward is the angry ocean. I'll call that the world
that we live in. You feel trapped. When Grant died, Kara and I both wondered, "How do we

move on? Will we ever laugh again? What will we do for the holidays? Birthdays? Vacations?". We had no answers and we quickly realized that we did not have to answer those questions all at once. We just needed to take one small step at a time. As far as that first question goes, we couldn't see a way to move forward initially. God did. He has parted the waves multiple times in the last 41 days. That's what He does. When there seems to be no way, He will make a way. There are a lot of people in our circle, not just us, that have experienced great pain and loss. I pray that on those tough days, as hard as it can be sometimes, we will look to Him. He will provide an escape. A way out. A step forward.

Days of Praise: Day #12
"So I will bless You as long as I live; I will lift up my hands in Your name." Psalm 63:4

Yesterday, I had to go get my bus driver's (one of my many hats as a coach) physical renewed. One of the questions I had to fill out in the waiting room was "how many children?" Simple question, right? Last year I would've answered it without even thinking about it. But this year? I had to pause for a second or two. I was caught off guard. I will always have four children, but the fact that I had to pause made me realize that things will never quite be the same for our family.

2020. Uncertainty. Chaos. Covid. Loss of a child. Who could've seen this coming? Our God knew. He's not surprised. Not shaken. Not caught off guard. He's in control. He has been since the beginning of time. Our world seems to be spinning out of control at times. But things aren't falling apart. They're falling into place. If you can claim that, then you will have confidence that the world will not win. That's why in the midst of this crazy year, we can still lift our hands in praise. That's why our family will not be crushed by Grant's death. It will grow stronger through His grace and mercy. Some days are not easy. Sometimes they are awfully hard. But He knew that too. And that is why He is right by our side. Let faith arise.

Days of Praise: Day #13

"Above all else, guard your heart, for everything you do flows from it."   Proverbs 4:23

What a day. More on that tomorrow. I'm literally typing this on my phone with its flashlight. Still no power. Mrs. Bridges , please excuse my grammatical errors. I will be happy to diagram each sentence perfectly when the lights come back on. At least I'll try.

I absolutely love the song "Waymaker". I can close my eyes and hear my sweet friend Lyn Westafer singing the solo on this song at church. Over our lifetime we have prayed so many prayers. Prayers for big things. Small things. Ordinary things. Miraculous things. Honestly, they're all small to our all powerful God, even if they seem so big to us. Many times He grants us what we pray for. But sometimes He chooses not to. He doesn't always answer them in the way we think He should. We may think He's not listening. But I know He always hears our prayers. That's one of His promises.

For two days in September, He made a way. He worked a miracle. He kept his promise. He was a light in the darkness. Just not in the way we wanted. The 36 hours of waiting in the hospital was definitely the hardest thing we have ever gone through. It seemed like an eternity. But God was moving. He was working. He was not still. I've never seen him face to face, but I've seen enough of Him in my life to believe Him and to trust Him.

And then I think of him. All we know of him is that he's a 62 year old man from the Carolina's. He had waited months, possibly years. Waiting for that phone call and knowing that several hours later he would be receiving a new heart. A new chance at life. Our sadness was his happiness.

Our God is the greatest heart surgeon of all time. He touches, heals and mends hearts. He has a 100% success rate. Through our 62 year old man from the Carolinas, He worked physically to give him a new heart. Through Grant, He worked eternally to give him a new heart. Through us , he worked and continues to work emotionally and spiritually, one day at a time, to give us a new heart. Thank you God. That is why we worship You.

Days of Praise: Day #14

"When you pass through the waters, I will be with you; and through the rivers, they shall not overwhelm you; when you walk through the fire you shall not be burned, and the flame shall not consume you." Isaiah 43:2

What a crazy morning on Thursday. Who would've imagined we would've had a tropical storm warning in Greenville, SC? 2020 continues to bring us unexpected events. We live in a very wooded community. I woke up early last Thursday to the sound of some very strong gusts of wind. I would hold my breath for several seconds after every gust just waiting to hear a tree or limb fall. Knowing that at any instant our power may go out. Then 8:15 am. Darkness. We all really take electricity and power for granted. Even though we are so reliant on it. We borrowed a generator from a friend this morning to try to save all of the food in our freezer. Got it all hooked up. Both of our refrigerators and our wi-fi (which Zack was most interested in restoring) came to life again. Not 30 minutes later, the power came back on. Oh well.

The neurosurgeon on call at GHS Memorial on Sept. 15, 2020 came into Grant's room on Tuesday night after the accident. I don't recall his name. If you know a neurosurgeon or are one or are married to one, please don't take this the wrong way. They are very to the point. Not much sunshine. It's okay though. We would rather have someone who is brilliant in this situation over someone who could just make us feel better. He basically said that Grant's injuries were unrecoverable. Talk about a gut punch. Basically in the eyes of science, no hope. The only reason he would be kept for the next day, monitored, and given one last neurological test the next night was because of his young age. A little hope.

BUT, and this is a HUGE but. We continued to believe that God could heal Grant. God created science. He is bigger than science and doctors. And He was completely able. And if He was willing, he would've done it. We had FULL confidence in Him even up until 10:16 pm on Wednesday, Sept. 16. He chose not to. That would be such a hard thing to swallow for a lot of people. And it was for us too at first.

HOWEVER, God has given us so many blessings and things in our life. Sometimes he chooses to take away some things as well. I had a job taken away from me before, but nothing in comparison to this loss. I'm not sure we could lose something so special to us like this. BUT, if you can't praise God in the valleys then you can't really praise Him on the mountains. We will continue to praise Him in the storm. He is still able. And always will be. Amen.

October 31, 2020:" Just sitting here in the backyard waiting for the fire to go out. Grant used to always brag about the stash of candy he got and at the same time complain about the "trash" candy he got after trick or treating. Grant's rants as we would always call them. His car still sits in front of our house. The basketball court is just below where I'm sitting. Oh, we just miss him so much. We are so happy that he's in heaven, but we still miss our tall red head. We know God's taking care of him now. Still hurts. Basketball season starts on Monday. Tough weekend for us."

Days of Praise: Day #15
"Therefore if anyone is in Christ, the new creation has come. The old is gone and the new is here." 2 Corinthians 5:17

Today is bittersweet for our family. There is excitement that today is the first official day of basketball practice. My 26th. My mind was racing last night in bed thinking about practice plans and schedules. There is also a sadness in that Grant won't be practicing today. Since we were at different schools, I only got to see a handful of Grant's games. Most people would tell me at his games, "How can you just sit there quietly and watch, you're a coach." I always felt like my role at his games was as a father and not as a coach. Now when we got home....Lol. When I would get home after practice and Grant would be sitting on the couch, I would always ask him how his practice went. Most of the time I got the typical teenager answer, "Good". I would then ask him if he had taken a charge on defense in practice. That was always a "No" or sometimes an "Almost". Grant was not one to sacrifice his slender body. I would like to think that he would've taken one today. Just this once. I'll have to ask him sometime down the road.

Today, I'm also thankful that Jesus DID sacrifice his body to save us from our sins. Without that selfless act, our family could not have the hope that we will reunite with Grant one day. This basketball season will be a little different for us. I will miss those conversations about practice. We will miss seeing him play. I know he'll still be watching. Great are You Lord.

Days of Praise: Day #16

"Lord, show us the Father, and that will be enough for us." John 14:8

Enough. The definition of enough is "as much as is required." Two things that were constant "conversations" between Grant and me were that I didn't think he ate very well and that he didn't get enough sleep. Didn't meet the necessary requirements in my opinion. If it weren't for Sara Kate (aka SK) and Jana (SK's mother), he probably wouldn't have eaten breakfast most mornings. SK would always pack some extra breakfast just for Grant. There were also many (maybe many is an exaggeration but it strengthens my story) nights where I would be awakened by Grant yelling at a screen playing Fortnite with his friends. I would walk downstairs and "gently" tell him to go to bed. He would always say "I'm good." when it came to nutrition and sleep. In all honesty though, probably no different than when I was 16. Lol. Except I had no screen. Don't all 16 year olds think they know it all? Many of you probably just said "Amen".

Even as a 48 year old, am I really that different from my 16 year old son? I know what I need. I'm experienced, right? I should be able to tell God what is best for my life, correct? Our prayers are often dictated by what WE think we need. Only GOD knows what we need, however. Sometimes they match. Sometimes they don't. Regardless of what we think, He will always be enough. In all situations. The things that are probably not enough in my life are my prayer life, my praise, and my gratitude. Peace to the broken. Faith for the widow. Hope for the orphan. Strength for the weak.

Days of Praise: Day #17

"Then great multitudes came to Him, having with them the lame, blind, mute, maimed and many others: and they laid them down at Jesus' feet, and He healed them." Matthew 15:30

Today is probably one of the greatest examples of the freedom that we enjoy living in a democracy. Hopefully, we all exercised our freedom in voting for the leaders not only for our country, but for our local communities. Even if every one of the candidates I voted for today don't see victory tonight, I have full confidence that my God will always be in control. That's one of His great promises.

My God also promises that we can take every burden and concern in this life and come and lay them at his feet. What an awesome promise. True freedom. Our past. Our mistakes. Our doubts. Our fears. Every single one of them. None are too large. None are too small or too trivial. I would like to think that Grant is sitting down at His feet tonight. The idea that the prayers I pray tonight and lay at Jesus' feet are seen and heard by Grant is so comforting to me.

I have prayed for months on my drive to Pickens HS for unity in our country. Most people would say that's impossible. Those people must have not met my God. He is able. He is the possible when all else seems impossible. Thank you God for giving me the hope and the freedom of the ultimate victory. Whoever is the elected president is temporary. My God is eternal.

Days of Praise: Day #18
"For if we have been planted together in the likeness of His death, we shall also be in the likeness of his resurrection. ". Romans 6:5

I was asked by Rikki Owens, our volleyball coach at Pickens HS, to give the girls a pre game speech before they leave tomorrow to go compete for a state title. What an honor. I've taught several of the girls. Even the ones I haven't taught, I've developed such a sweet friendship. Such a special group of young ladies. Rikki and Pamela Clarkson, assistant volleyball coach at PHS, are such great coaches and I am so happy to call them friends.

Grant LOVED competition. He was all about it. I know he will be looking down tomorrow night and pulling for Blue Flame volleyball. Win or lose, however, these girls are winners in my book. The only victory that is guaranteed is through His name. No chance of losing. Such confidence. Such hope. Game. Set. Match. Go Blue Flame!

Days of Praise: Day #19

"I sought the Lord, and he answered me; he delivered me from all my fears. Those who look to him are radiant; their faces are never covered with shame." Psalm 34:4-5

Many days we have things delivered "to" us. Amazon, UPS, USPS, FedEx....especially with Christmas right around the corner. But how often are we delivered "from" things? Probably many more times then we realize. Many times we don't see them until after the fact. God is constantly working behind the scenes in our life. As hard as it may seem to realize, He's working in our country right now. He never rests. He is never silent. The problem is that we get so busy that the world drowns out His voice in our lives.

Grant was like most teenage boys. He enjoyed playing video games. Kara and I constantly struggled with how much was too much, especially with a ten year old little brother watching him so intently. He often didn't hear us calling him upstairs to come eat because he was wearing headphones. We would get so agitated at times. I wonder how God feels when we do the same thing to Him. We can't hear Him because of all of the noise in our life. We're never quiet long enough to listen. Take time this weekend and be quiet. Look to Him. That problem or pain that you're going through...He may be in the process of delivering you "from" it. "Oh taste and see, that the Lord is good; blessed is the one who takes refuge in Him." Psalm 34:8

Days of Praise: Day #20

"Come and see what the Lord has done, the desolations He has brought on earth. He makes wars cease to the ends of the earth. He breaks the bow and shatters the spear; He burns the chariots with fire." Psalm 46:8-9

During the initial stages of Covid and quarantine, Jake mentioned wanting to build a fire pit in our backyard. Since we were all just sitting around in the house, we thought it would be a fun project. We called it Jake's "senior project". He planned it completely and built it with a little help here and there. Grant and his friends would like to hang out by the fire pit, even though a fire in the spring didn't make much sense. It was neat to look out into the backyard and see them just huddled around each other. He really loved his friends.

Fire can really have a dual purpose. If it is controlled, it can provide warmth and comfort to those in its presence. Who doesn't enjoy a good s'more? Left uncontrolled, it can destroy and cause havoc. It can burn down houses, forests and whole communities in a flash. Our world seems like it is always in a perpetual state of uncontrolled fire. Pain, panic, loss all around. If there is anything that I have learned, it is that there is not an elected official, a policy or law that will fix it. Only He can. You see, fire has more than just physical purposes. God has placed a fire, a spiritual fire, in us that cannot be quenched. It is THAT fire that He wants to be uncontrolled. Uncontrolled by the world. It is through believers reaching out to the lost and broken of our world and showing them a hope that they can only find through Him. His fire doesn't destroy lives. It saves them.

Days of Praise: Day #21

"The Lord is my strength and my shield; in Him my heart trusts, and I am helped; my heart exults, and with my song I give thanks to Him." Psalm 28:7

Trust. It takes a long time to build but only a short time to destroy. Back in the spring, Grant took an interest in playing golf. One of his buddies worked at a golf course so he basically could play for free. He didn't have his own set of golf clubs so he started borrowing mine. I would always tell him that when he got home to put the clubs in the garage and not keep them in his Durango. The hatch on it would not lock. Golf clubs are not cheap. One day in the summer, I felt like going to hit golf balls. I went out to the garage but could not find my clubs. I called Grant who was at a friend's house. He said he still had them in the back of his car and would bring them home. Several minutes later I get a frantic phone call. "Dad, they're not there. I'm so sorry. I'll get a job. I'll replace them." I have to admit, my heart dropped a bit and I was not very joyful at the time. In my mind I was preparing my trust "conversation" for when Grant got home. About five minutes later, I got another call from Grant. "Dad, they're in the back of Brody's car. I forgot I had put them in there." Disaster avoided. Maybe not the conversation though.

The problem with trust on this side of heaven is that we are all human. People and things are going to let us down. Period. That's our nature. Often it is unintentional but nonetheless hurtful. Years of building trust in someone can come crashing down in a moment. There is only one person who will never betray our trust. Jesus. He'll never let us down or fail us. If you put your trust in politics, your job, your family or people in general, at some point you're going to get disappointed. And at some point you're going to disappoint someone else. The great thing about God though is that when we disappoint Him, he is quick to forgive and restore. Even greater than that, however, is that He will NEVER disappoint us.

Days of Praise: Day #22

"Then you will know the truth, and the truth shall set you free." John 8:32

"I want the truth." "You can't handle the truth." Famous lines from a great movie. Some people have a hard time with honesty and some do not. Grant certainly did not mind

sharing his thoughts about things in his life that he did not like. Don't get me wrong, he had a sweet, caring heart but he also had his sassy side. It was quite obvious to us when Grant disapproved of some circumstance or obstacle in his life. He would use such terms of endearment as, "That's trash." Or "Garbage." Or "Piece of junk." He was a very good student but many times these expressions came out in regards to something he had to do at school, like Spanish or Physics. At times, his brutal honesty about life matched his fiery red hair. We loved that part of him and often laughed about it.

Truth in today's world is often muddled. People like to live in the gray, because in the gray there are no standards or if there are, you can move that standard to fit your actions and behaviors. If you don't like the truth or being held to a standard, then just make up your own. Truth can change depending on who you are tuning into or the current trends. It's fluid. Whatever makes you feel good about yourself.

Man, has the world sold us a lie or what? There IS a truth and a standard. It's God's Word. It is just as alive and applicable today as the day it was written. Yes, it contains a lot of history. Don't leave out the present and the future, though. From beginning to end and everything in between. It provides for us a standard that is both indelible and irrefutable. Dealing with pain or loss? Open the cover. Feeling abandoned or alone? Start reading. Whatever season of life you are in right now, His word provides freedom. It provides hope. It provides truth. One cannot come into the presence of God and His Word without being miraculously changed. THAT is the truth. The whole truth. And nothing but the truth. So help us God.

Days of Praise: Day #23

"Draw near to God, and He will draw near to you." James 4:8

July 1996. Kara and I had just been married a few days earlier. We were laying in bed early one morning in the Bahamas on our honeymoon. The phone rings. It's Kara's mom. Whose mom calls on their daughter's honeymoon? This was before cellphones were the norm. My first thought was, "What have I gotten myself into?" She wanted to know if we were okay because of the hurricane. What hurricane? We're on our honeymoon. There was a TV in the room but we had not turned it on. We turned it on that morning and sure enough there she was, Hurricane Bertha, heading right towards the Bahamas. I walked down to the front desk of our hotel to ask if we should be alarmed. The lady said to me (in my best Bohemian accent), "Oh no, hurricane never hit Bahamas." Not very reassuring. Lady, I think all of the hurricanes I've seen on the news in my life have affected the Bahamas. Whatever you say. It worked out as we departed the Bahamas about a day before it arrived. I didn't call back to see if she was right or not.

2020 has been one of the most active years on record for tropical activity. Anyone shocked? I've compared Grant's accident to a hurricane before. Just like the hurricane on our honeymoon, we were unaware it was coming. No warning. What do you do when a hurricane, no matter small or large, shows up in your life unexpectedly? Go to the center, the eye of the storm. That is where you will find God. That is where you will find peace and calm. Kara and I could've lived in the outer bands of the hurricane where the rain and wind reside. We made a commitment to each other from the very beginning that we would move to the center. The eyewall is the outer band of the eye. It is where you will find the strongest forces of the storm. There were days, and still are, where we drifted towards the eyewall. On those days, when the rain and wind picked up, we chose to re-center. How do you do that when you are getting battered on all sides? Pray. Even when you don't have the words. Sing. Even if you can't sing. Open His Word. Even if you never have before. Draw near to God. Even when you don't feel close to him. He will draw near to you.

November 15, 2020 (Kara's words): "A friend brought me some breakfast bread this weekend. It reminded me of the last time she did that; the day after Grant passed into heaven. On that day back in September, she felt God telling her to bring us some bread and she tried to ignore Him thinking it probably wasn't a good time and she would probably be in the way and we wouldn't need cinnamon bread anyway. But despite her hesitation, she showed up on our front porch early that morning. She didn't know she was arriving right after I had to be the strongest I have ever been in my life as I told my 9 year old that his brother was now in heaven. She didn't know that I needed to simply fall into her arms and be held as the tears came. She didn't know it wasn't the bread I needed but her comfort. She didn't know, but God did!

I have countless stories of people showing up! Things like a chair in the hospital (I love to tell that story) or a vacuum cleaner or an orange blanket or a tray of nuggets or a candle or a package of bacon, etc. Our friends, family, church and community have overwhelmed us! We have appreciated every call, text, card, visit, flower, meal, gift, donation, gift card and hug.

The next time someone you know is hurting, there are probably no right words to say but go ahead and make the call, send the card, go visit or take them the bread. It is probably just what they need!"

Days of Praise: Day #24
"Let not your heart be troubled. You believe in God; believe in me also." John 14:1

I basically have chosen to live in self-pity the past couple of weeks. It wasn't a very productive choice. It never really is but it's so easy to slip into when dealing with loss in your life. When the devil sees you on the top of the mountain, he's going to do anything in his power to knock you down. I allowed him to do it even though I had the greatest power ever imaginable to defeat him.

I struggled emotionally for several weeks after Grant's death. The overwhelming support of family, friends and God was really the only thing that got me through those first few weeks. There wasn't much time to just sit around and think with all of the meals and visitors. I knew those things would eventually slow down. As I went back to work, I was in a very good spot spiritually and emotionally. Some normalcy started to come back to my life. I still grieved for Grant but I had things to do that gave me a distraction. Basketball started and things seemed well in my life.

I found out that I had to be quarantined from work on Friday, Nov. 6 because of close contact with a co-worker. Since I had no symptoms, I was given the option to continue working as normal. Of course, I started feeling bad the next day. I debated getting tested. We were about to start week 2 of basketball practice. I didn't have time to be out. I finally decided it was the right thing to do to be tested. I went to get tested on Monday, Nov. 9. I was out of work and basketball practice until the results came back. I found out on

Wednesday, Nov. 11 that I was positive. I could not return to work until Wednesday, Nov. 18. I never had real severe symptoms but I still did not feel like doing much other than lying around the house. Time to just sit and think. At this point, I think the devil came at me full force. Poor pitiful Jeff. Your life is so hard. He kept saying these things to me and I allowed myself to entertain them. Instead of focusing on all of the good things in my life, I settled on the negative things.

I have always tried to teach my players that life is 10% of what happens to you and 90% of how you respond. For the two weeks I was out, I had it backwards. I focused on that which I could not control instead of that which I could. It's such an easy trap if you do not keep your eyes on Jesus. He never left me or moved away from me. Guess what. If you don't feel close to God, guess who moved? I realize that now as I have gone back to work. Tuesday was two months since Grant passed away. It still hurts and sometimes does not feel real. There will always be days like that. My prayer for myself and for others is that when those days come that we will not allow the evil one to take our eyes off of Jesus as I did the last two weeks. We have the power to always keep us from doing that. We just have to choose to use it.

Days of Praise: Day #25
"I give thanks to you, O Lord my God, with my whole heart, and I will glorify your name forever." Psalm 86:12

Continually amazed by the goodness of God. Grant played for TR Elite AAU growing up and then played the last two years for Wade Hampton HS. Josh Mills (basketball coach at Travelers Rest HS) and Reggie Choplin (basketball coach at Wade Hampton HS) are both life long friends to me. They played tonight and there was a moment of silence tonight for Grant. I had a game at Eastside tonight with my Pickens team so I couldn't be there. Someone sent us the video. Our family was greatly touched and appreciative. We are so thankful that Grant had the opportunity to play for both programs.

November 25, 2020: "Tomorrow will be tough. We will have one less plate at the Thanksgiving table. We love tradition but decided this holiday season to do something different. Kara, Callie, Jake, Zack and I are in the NC mountains for a few days. We will eat our "traditional" turkey lunch at Daniel Boone Inn. We still miss Grant so much but he will be with us in spirit and in our hearts tomorrow. Fly high Grant!"

Days of Praise: Day #26

"Let the peace of Christ rule in your hearts, since as members of one body you were called to peace. And be thankful." Colossians 3:15

Nov. 28, 2019. It was a typical Thanksgiving day for the Harrelson family. As we got going that morning, we did the traditional things. We turned on the Macy's Thanksgiving Day Parade (much better non-Covid I must say). Kara was in the kitchen preparing green bean or pea casserole (I can't remember which one) to take to lunch. The six of us got into the van and drove to Kara's parents as we had for so many consecutive years. We had a great time eating and fellowshipping with one another. We had no idea at the time that one year later there would only be five of us getting into the van on Thanksgiving day. We love our Thanksgiving traditions but decided this year to do something different. Instead of driving to the Blocks, we drove a "little" further to the NC mountains for the holidays. Today was really the first holiday without Grant. We had a nice traditional Thanksgiving lunch at the Daniel Boone Inn in Boone. We missed having six around the table but we had a great time. A former player's mom sent me a poem this morning entitled "The Empty Chair Prayer" that at the end said, "For those gathered around a table that has an empty chair, Oh Lord, comfort their hearts—we know that you are able, and let them know that this year, there's another chair at Heaven's table." I really had not thought of it that way. It made me smile. Oh God, if there happened to be ham on that table today, please don't put pineapple on it. Grant really didn't like that. And he wasn't afraid to tell you about it.

Days of Praise: Day #27

"For the mountains may depart and the hills be removed, but my steadfast love shall not depart from you, and my covenant of peace shall not be removed." Isaiah 54:10

Hills and valleys. We've all been there, right? On Sept, 14, 2020, I can't remember if I was on the mountain or not. But 24 hours later, I was definitely in the valley. I was reminded of the notion of hills and valleys on our trip to the NC mountains for Thanksgiving this past weekend. Driving up, we could look up and see God's wonderful creation of mountains. When we went to Grandfather Mountain on Friday, we could look down and see the beauty in the valleys below. When we are on top of the mountain, it is easy to forget the valley that we just came through. When we seem to be stuck in the valley, it is also easy to forget the mountain that we were just on top of. The thing we have to remember is that no matter our elevation, that God still reigns supreme. He is there for us no matter where life takes us. We are never alone. So much easier to feel when we're on top, but no different when we feel we're on bottom. He is God at every point. That is what He promises. I believe in all His promises. I believe that He is taking supreme care of Grant. We miss him but we know he is in the best hands possible.

Days of Praise: Day #28
10 So do not fear, for I am with you;do not be dismayed, for I am your God.I will strengthen you and help you;I will uphold you with my righteous right hand.

Isaiah 41:10 | NIV

I really can't explain what today felt like. Two months ago I experienced one of the darkest days of my life. No parent expects to outlive their child. It's not something you can prepare for. It's not the natural order of life. We only survived it by the overwhelming support and love from our family and friends. We had no idea that on Dec 1st that God would ask us to provide the same love and support for one of our dearest friends' families who would lose one of their children. Our oldest son Jake was going to share an apartment with one of his closest friends in the fall. My heart truly aches for my son tonight. It also aches tremendously for his friend's family.

December 2, 2020: "This Saturday, Dec. 5th would've been Grant's 17th birthday. We struggled with how to celebrate but then we wanted to come up with a way to help others. We decided to buy 17 basketballs and donate to a toy drive in Pickens. We would love it if others would choose to donate a basketball to any local toy drive for Christmas. There are toy drives at Bon Secours and Greer Relief. Any toy drive would be greatly appreciated. We would love for you to send or post pictures.

Days of Praise: Day #29
"Every word of God proves true; he is a shield to those who take refuge in him."
Proverbs 30:5

Our hearts have been broken the past 24 hours for Chris and Kim Hall. Their son Eli, one of Jake's closest friends, has joined our son Grant in heaven. Unexpectedly. No warning. We have loved the Halls for many years and have spent many precious moments with them. Who knew that two months ago that they would be there for us and that yesterday those roles would be reversed? Only God knew.

In 2020, the world would tell us that there are no absolute truths. I'm sorry but I will have to disagree with that idea. With the news of Eli's passing, have we been angry? ABSOLUTELY. Just as we were two months ago. Have we questioned God? ABSOLUTELY. Have we felt lost and abandoned at times? ABSOLUTELY. However, do we serve a mighty God who can handle all of that? MOST ABSOLUTELY. His strength is perfect when ours is gone. It starts when ours ends. And that is why we have hope when things seem hopeless. Joy when all we can seem to find are tears. I can only imagine the smile on Grant's face yesterday when Eli arrived. Finally someone familiar to play one on one with. Praise God and please continue to pray for the Hall's and Harrelson's.

Days of Praise: Day #30
"You will be enriched in every way so that you can be generous on every occasion, and through your generosity will result in thanksgiving to God." 2 Corinthians 9:11

Overwhelmed doesn't even begin to describe our feelings towards our friends and community this evening. We knew this year would've been a very tough year of firsts without Grant. Thanksgiving, basketball season, birthday, Christmas. We really weren't sure how we would handle the above. Our support system of God, friends, family, church and community members have truly kept us afloat as a family. Grant's 17th birthday would've been in two days. For Grant's birthday we decided to use it as an opportunity to give back and serve others. 17 basketballs for 17 years of life that we could donate to a local toy drive for Christmas. Oh how we have been blessed and overwhelmed by those who have come beside us in this venture. We pray that a simple gift of a basketball at Christmas time would provide joy and hope to those who receive it. Grant would've definitely approved. We serve an awesome God.

Days of Praise: Day #31
"Each one must give as he has decided in his heart, not reluctantly or under compulsion, for God loves a cheerful giver. And God is able to make all grace abound

to you, so that having all sufficiency in all things at all times, you may abound in every good work." 2 Corinthians 9:6-8

December 5, 2003. What an amazing day for our family. To use a basketball term, it was the day that Kara and I went from playing man to man defense to zone defense. 3 wonderful children (with #4 coming much later.) I still remember looking at that little red fuzz on top of Grant's head. What a great day. A true gift from God.

It still doesn't feel quite real that he is not here today to celebrate his 17th birthday. As I have said before, as this day was approaching Kara and I were unsure of how this day might look. I saw a post on social media about a toy drive in Pickens happening today. Kara came up with the idea of donating 17 basketballs, for his 17 years, to this cause. We asked our friends to donate a ball as well this Christmas season in memory of Grant. Man, did we ever get what we asked for. I'm not sure there will be any more basketballs on store shelves in the Upstate. Amazing simply does not describe it.

Grant's story continues to live on. Tammy Anthony (assistant softball coach at Pickens HS and owner of Heidi's restaurant in Pickens), who is heading up the toy drive in Pickens today, made a comment that she wishes she could tell each child who gets a basketball today the blessing they are receiving. They will never know Grant but through the simple gift of a basketball, they may receive a little happiness and joy today. The generosity of so many people has really caused me to examine my life. I have a story. You have a story. That story may need to be heard by someone in your life. Your gift to them may not be a basketball. It might be a simple act of kindness. A hug. A phone call. A conversation. Don't let this day go by without giving something of yourself to someone in need. Happy Birthday Grant!

December 5, 2020: "What a tremendous day on Grant's 1st birthday celebration in heaven. The posts and messages we've received from people donating basketballs in his memory have been amazing. I would be typing for hours thanking everyone who has helped in this cause. You guys have meant so much to us. More than you'll ever imagine. At last count (rough count), over 200 balls have been donated so far. We are overwhelmed by the goodness of God and his people. We are truly blessed. Thank you all."

Days of Praise: Day #32

"Bear one another's burdens, and fulfill the law of Christ." Galatians 6:2

I've only been to a few funerals in my lifetime. I know that as I get older that will change. We had two very godly men in our church pass away in the past week. One was in his mid 80's and one was 98. So many years of great testimony and service to God. I'm sure they could tell story after story about their kids and grandkids. I love each family dearly and I grieve with them in their loss. I hate that I wasn't able to attend the funerals of these men. The last two funerals I have attended have hit me a little different though. The pain and sorrow is no different for families depending on the age of the deceased but at times I still can't wrap my heart and head around celebrating the lives of two teenage boys in the prime of their lives. Parents left wondering what could've been. Would our grandkids have that same flowing red hair?

Obviously, one of those teen boys was my own 16 year old son, Grant. The other was the 19 year old son of Chris and Kim Hall, Eli. Chris and I have been lifelong friends. We grew up together at Taylors First Baptist Church and swimming on the Rusty Brook swim team as teens. The Halls and Harrelsons became close friends as we both got married and began to have kids. Callie was our first and a few years older but Jake and Grant were right at the same age as Luke and Eli. Grant and Eli naturally gravitated towards each other as did Jake and Luke. Chris and I have always shared a bond with music. We sang together in the youth choir 30 years ago and continue to this day in the adult choir at TFBC. Kim worked as a nurse at Kara's school for several years. Ozzy has become a perfect companion for Zack. Our families just fit together. We have great memories of our families growing up together.

Neither family could ever imagine what this fall would hold for each of us. We've always felt that we could call on each other no matter what. "No matter what" started in early September with Grant's accident and death. The Hall's were nothing short of amazing for us. The hands and feet of God. I didn't think we could ever repay them. Until this past week. I had asked Chris to sing at Grant's funeral. At first he wasn't sure if he could get through it emotionally. I told him I completely understood. A short time later, he called me and said he would love to. When I got the call from Chris about singing in Eli's service, I immediately had some of the same hesitations as Chris had. But it didn't take long for me to convince myself that I would be honored. Kara was right there by Kim's side the rest of the week after Eli's passing. You see, that's what friends do. That's what we as Christians should do. Share each other's burdens. Pick each other up when one of us falls. Comfort each other through loss. Even when you don't know the words to say. Even this week, I have struggled with what to say to Kim and Chris even though I know exactly what they are going through. There are no words. And that's okay.

As Chris and I were up on stage yesterday about to sing together, I was thinking about the new bond we now share. One that no parent would ever want to face. Certainly not alone. The loss of a child. Our love of the Halls has always been strong but it has become rock solid through these past few months. If you're feeling down today or any day in the days leading to Christmas, find someone to serve. Be the hands and feet of Jesus. Give of yourself even when it may feel uncomfortable. Fulfill the law of Christ. Great will be your reward.

December 10, 2020: "We were really blown away this morning as the faculty and staff at Kara's school surprised us with a tree planted in front of the school in memory of Grant. The picture on the plaque was taken when Grant was a 4K student at her school. The rocks were painted by some of her staff and students. God is so good and he keeps reminding us of the goodness and love of his people."

December 11, 2020: "Update: 117 balls were donated this morning alone at PHS FCA. That puts the total of the donations I'm aware of at over 500. God is good."

December 18, 2020: "Shoutout to Pickens Middle School girls and boys basketball teams for donating basketballs in memory of Grant for Christmas. Thank you so much to Coach Smith (girls coach) and Coach Wakefield (boys coach). Officially puts the number of balls to over 700. Overwhelming. God is so good. Go Blue Flame!"

December 18, 2020: "Tomorrow we leave for Disney. Christmas will be different without Grant. I took Zack this afternoon to get a haircut. We talked about our trip on the way. He mentioned that Grant was always his roller coaster riding buddy. Crazy how small little things bring a tear to your eye. I guess I might have to step up and fill that role. Though at my age, I like my feet on the ground. Lol.

December 23, 2020:" Night #4 at Disney. This place is pretty amazing. I've seen lots of shirts saying this place is home. Even magical. Drove to the grocery store tonight and heard the song "there's no place like home for the holidays". Jake made the comment tonight that it didn't really feel like Christmas. I had to agree. Not that we have not had a great time. We certainly have. But it's not home. It's not our tradition. I shed a few tears driving back to our resort. We enjoyed the mountains for Thanksgiving. We celebrated Grant's birthday with an absolutely amazing gift of basketballs in his memory. Over 700. But there's something about Christmas. So many memories. Waking up to see what Santa brought. Going to grandparents for presents, lunch and supper. Even in the extreme activity and joy of Disney, we still miss Grant so much. It has felt weird at times to tell the park attendants that we have five. We were six for so long. Just missing him tonight."

December 25, 2020: "This post doesn't have a number. For weeks after losing Grant, I posted almost every day and gave it a number. I think I ran out of words. It's been a little over 3 months since Grant's accident. Some days it seems like 3 days ago. Some days it seems like 3 years ago. Today is Christmas Day 2020. What a year. First of all and most importantly, Happy Birthday Jesus! Without this day, there would be no joy. No happiness. No hope. Praise God that He had a plan. God created us as humans. Which means he instilled in us all of the full spectrum of human emotions. From the brightest to the darkest. Our family has trekked through the whole range in the last few months. Thankfully, He has been there for us through all of them. As we wake up this morning, it will be the first Christmas morning for us as a family of 5 in a while. Not easy. So used to 6. Christmas morning holds so many memories and excitement. As excited as we will be this morning, it pales in comparison to the birthday party in heaven that Grant will experience today. Happy Birthday Jesus! We miss you Grant.

A New Year

December 31, 2020: *"What a difference a year makes. Last year at this time we were ringing in the new year with friends. This year we are with those same friends...virtually. On a Zoom call. 2020 was going to be a momentous year in the life of our family. Jake would be graduating high school and entering college. Going to prom. All the things that parents look forward to celebrating with their children. March 13, 2020 came. Friday the 13th. Man did it live up to it. The world was shut down. Surely it wouldn't last long. Then March Madness was canceled. Our annual Spring Break trip to Hilton Head was canceled. Jake's prom was canceled. His graduation was far from traditional. His entrance into college was delayed a month. We had just started feeling a small sense of normal by moving Jake into Clemson in early September. Then Sept. 15, 2020 came. The most challenging and difficult day of my life up to that point. Out of nowhere. I still vividly remember my father in law on our front porch at somewhere around 1:00 am telling us Grant had been involved in an accident with Parker. There's no way that could be real. Must be a bad dream. Looking back now, it was a gift from God that we got to spend 36 hours by his side, even though we now know his chances of survival were slim. We cried, prayed and sang over him. We needed that. Then the news of his organs being donated. God always knows what you need when you need it. The past few months have seemed like days and decades at times. There hasn't been a day since then that we haven't shed a tear or two or had some small remembrance of him. It's not something you ever get over completely. There won't be a day where we will finally say we're glad we finally got through this. But we serve a mighty God who has and will continue to sustain us in the days, weeks, months and years to come. I pray that this coming year that we will continue to lean on and rely on God as a family. He has never failed us and He promises that He never will."*

January 28, 2021: *"I've been busy with basketball season. Been a tough year. I hurt for our players. It's been a constant stop and start. Not ideal. I've tried to preach all year. Control what you can control. Doesn't make it any easier. There are still constant reminders of Grant not being with us. I looked forward to seeing him play at least a few games. I watch FSU basketball and I constantly look over to the couch. He would've been right there. Now he's not. It's just tough. I miss him so much. I know God has a plan. His ways are better than ours. I may not understand now but when I see Jesus I will."*

March 4, 2021: "Today was one of those days. One of those days where you're not really looking forward to the things you have to do but know you have to. Almost 6 months after Grant's death, we finally went back to the mortuary to get his urn and take it to our church to place in his final earthly resting place. Kara and I held it together pretty well. Was not easy though. One of those reminders that will continue to happen. Thankful that we can lean on God.

We then helped my dad take my mom to her neurologist appointment. It's so hard to see my mom, who a year ago was playing tennis 3-4 times a week, to suddenly not be able to walk on her own. We are praying that God would direct us to a clinic that can help her. The doctors at Prisma have been awesome. But they have not seen patients with what is causing my mom all of her issues. It is extremely rare. We will likely have to travel far away. Please pray for my dad. A lot has been put on him.

Tomorrow is Jake's 19th birthday. He and Callie came home tonight and ate dinner. It's times like tonight that make me miss Grant. We were six strong for so many years. We still are but in a different way now.

Please pray for me tomorrow morning. I'm speaking at PHS FCA. Talking about "Why does God allow bad things to happen to good people?" I've really wrestled with that for the past almost 6 months. Pray that God would speak through me."

March 15, 2021: "Tomorrow will be 6 months since Grant left this earth. Kind of hard to imagine it's been that long. We've learned a lot since then. We'll continue to learn. We'll continue to grieve. We'll continue to appreciate the almost 17 years we had with him on earth. He always loved March Madness. We have done a family bracket contest the last several years. He and I would watch every game that was on television. It was our time. It was kind of our thing. I will miss him not being with me this tournament.
One of the things God has taught me the past six months is to cherish the times we DID have together. And not to focus on the things we will miss. I'll be honest. That's really hard. Really hard. I'm sure over the next few weeks I'll look over to my right watching a game to make a comment and will be surprised he's not there. It was always just natural. I continue to go back to thinking that we really can't imagine going through the last 6 months without God on our side. His promises are true. Always have been. Always will be.
Psalm 23 was sung this past week in our service by Kevin and Scott. They sang the same song at Grant's funeral. I might've teared up a little. But the promise is true. "Even though I

walk through the valley of the shadow of death, I will fear no evil." We know where Grant is today. And we rejoice. We will see him again. He's just run ahead of us a little bit.

May 17, 2021: "Special evening tonight. Grant was awarded his basketball letter at Wade Hampton. Thank you Reggie Choplin for honoring him. He would've loved playing for you. We will forever miss seeing him play again."

June 9, 2021: "Growth. How do you measure it? We have kept up with our kids on the wall of our pantry. Kara says if we ever move that we're taking that piece of wood with us. At the top is Grant's last measurement. 05/18. He grew a good bit after that. There's an old Indian tale that the sighting of a red bird represents a loved one that has come back to visit. I've seen so many red birds in the past several months. I guess I've just been more aware. I know it's Grant. I saw one today while Jake and I were playing golf. He was probably saying he would've beaten both of us. Lol. We've learned so much about God in the last 9 months. The biggest thing I've learned is that He knows about losing a son. He watched his only son die. The pain that we've felt, He felt too. The joy that He felt being reunited with His son in heaven is the same joy that we will experience one day. We miss you Grant. But we'll see you again. And it will be spectacular."

June 20, 2021:" I've been very blessed with four wonderful children. I enjoyed going to Pelicans with Callie, Jake and Zack on not only Fathers Day but the first day of summer as well. It's been our tradition for years. They're such great kids. I love them dearly. It's tough to look at this picture without Grant in it, however. He was such a great kid too. But then I think about what his day must've been like. He got to say "Happy Father's Day" to our Heavenly Father. Days like today are both the hardest and the sweetest at the same time. Hard because we miss Grant. Sweet because he is in the presence of Jesus.

July 2, 2021: "Played golf this morning by myself. I'd rather play with others. But I enjoyed some quiet time with just myself. I honestly saw a red bird on almost every hole. Don't know if it was the same one. Doesn't matter. Even if I hit a wayward shot (or many), the sight of this bird made me smile every single time. Such a reminder of Grant. I almost feel like I stole from Pebble Creek. I only paid for one but two of us played today."

August 3, 2021: "Year 27 of the first day of school as a teacher. My journey from Year 1 has been pretty amazing. As I sat before my classes today for the first time, one of my students *asked me why I decided to teach. Kind of put me on the spot. He said he could never do it. I told him I felt that that is what I was called to do. I honestly believe that. Could I have gone into a profession that paid more money? Obviously. But I wouldn't trade any of the past 26 years as a teacher/coach for any amount of money. The relationships and special moments I have shared with my students and players are worth more to me than any dollar sign.*

As I planned my intro lesson this year, I had to make a few changes. This is the "first" school day in 17 years without Grant. I always show a picture of my family to my students. I wrestled with that this year. Kara and I wrestled with the question of "How many kids do you have?" for quite awhile. We both have since come to the answer that we have four: three here with us and one waiting on us. So I was open and honest with my students. It was good for me to get through that today.

I learned the other day that one of my HS teammates had passed away suddenly. It reminded me of how fragile life can be. We are not promised anything past the right now. We were not prepared for Grant to leave us just as Rod's family was not as well. I immediately thought of an old song that was popular in the 80's. Still applies today. Looking forward to what Year 27 has in store. I'm pretty sure it will be great."

August 9, 2021: " If you don't feel close to God, guess who moved? I heard this 30 years ago in a college Sunday school class at my church. I have been reminded of it the past few days and weeks. It could be that my circle of grief has slowly come back around to anger and bitterness. It's not something I planned nor desired. There really is no way to prepare for some of the small, sometimes insignificant, incidents of life that have reminded me of losing Grant almost a year ago. It may be that school is starting back up. It could be that when I look up in the back row of the balcony at church every Sunday, I see Grant's friends but not him. There have been lots of happy memories since September, but lately they've seemed to cause more pain than joy.

This would've been Grant's senior year. A definite milestone in anyone's life. Everyone remembers their senior year. We will miss out on senior pictures. Zack will take his "first day of school" picture alone this year. I know it would've happened next year when Grant would've been at college but it stings this year. Grant would've been the big man on campus once again. His senior year of basketball. Senior prom. Graduation. Tomorrow is the insurance settlement hearing from his accident. It has been hanging over our heads for almost eleven months. We still need to have his gravestone engraved. No way to really have final closure. If that's even possible.

Sitting in church yesterday morning, words were coming out of my mouth during the singing but I can't really say I felt them or even meant them. I'm just angry again. I feel like my prayers lately have been dry and stale. Just words. Not that God isn't listening. He hears every word. But my heart has not been right. I've gone back to trying to blame someone for Grant's death. Even God at times. The further away from God you move, the louder the enemy can be. You start to lose a little of the hope that you have always held to. Anger is definitely not my favorite emotion. I would much rather circle around back to joy.

As I listened to the sermon on Psalm 34 yesterday at church, I definitely felt convicted. Still angry and bitter, but convicted. So how do I take my anger and bitterness and turn it back into joy? How do I get back to hope? The problem is "I" can't do it. It is only through Him that I can. My only option is to move closer to Him. We often look for reasons or blame for our circumstances. Sometimes the only reason that bad things happen to good people is that we live in a broken world. God does not always reveal to us the whole picture. If he did, there would be no need for faith. What he does reveal, however, will always be sufficient. What we see now in part we will one day see in full.

I was preparing a lesson for my Life Group about a month ago on Job. I have always heard that God doesn't give us more than we can handle. Then I came across the following thought: Sometimes God gives us MORE than WE can handle because if WE could handle it then WE would not need HIM. Lord, I need you right now. I can't do this alone. I stand on your promises of **Psalm 34:17-18:**

"The righteous cry out and the Lord hears them; He delivers them from all of their troubles. The Lord is close to the brokenhearted and saves those who are crushed in spirit."

August 10, 2021: "God always knows what you need at the exact time you need it. I'm extremely blessed with a tremendous network of friends and family. I felt every single prayer today. Came across a great quote today. "I have come to learn that peace is not the absence of trial, trouble or torment but the presence of calm in them." (Don Meyer) Thank you God for providing peace and calm in the midst of loss. "

August 14, 2021: "*Wow. What a week. Life has a way of running you through the ringer. God has a way of reminding you of how good He is. Last Sunday I was in an angry/bitter stage in my life. Then to find out that FSU legend coach Bobby Bowden had passed away. Monday we found out our principal was leaving. Friday afternoon we found out we were going virtual starting Monday. Ugh.*

I watched a video this week of Ernie Johnson, sportscaster, talking to the Alabama football team. He said everyone's goal each day should be "to make someone's life better". I came across a Bobby Bowden quote as well. "Don't leave this earth with life unused". What a great reminder. It's not about us. We should model the same grace towards others that God has provided for us believers. When you come across those days where you feel like you can't find a reason to get up or live, find someone to serve. Make their life better. It might be just a phone call. It might just be a smile. It might just be your presence. It will make your struggles seem not so big.

God certainly reminded me this week of His goodness through the many prayers of my friends. My challenge to all who read this is to go out this week and show/remind others of His goodness. You never know what someone might need."

August 15, 2021: "*I've said all weekend, "control what you can control". Really not looking forward to going virtual tomorrow. God did not promise us that life would be without trials and challenges. He did promise us that through Him we would have the power to overcome whatever the world throws at us. I can always control my attitude and my heart.*

It's been easy to focus on Grant these last 11 months and the impact his death has had on me personally as a father. But there are four other people in our house that have had to deal with it as well. Kara and I both agreed early on to allow each of our children the freedom to grieve in the manner that they felt they needed. We had conversations but we did not push them in any certain direction. We found out that we all grieved and remembered Grant in our own unique ways. And that's okay. We will continue to remember Grant and still process last September the rest of our lives.

As we packed up Jake and Callie tonight to head back to Clemson something just hit me. As we have dealt with the loss of a son and brother, it has been easy to focus on Grant. I want to spend a few minutes focusing on my amazing family still here on Earth.

Kara. A true Proverbs 31 woman. The rock of our family. The loss of a son as a father was almost unbearable. I can't imagine the pain of a mother. She starts a new school year this week. She has certainly found her calling. She is incredible at what she does. I can't imagine a better leader of a school. I pray the Lord blesses her this year. I love you.

Callie. Our first born. Our only daughter. I know losing a sibling was tough. You handled it with such grace. Starting your senior year of college. Unbelievable. I know you don't like change but I know you are grounded in God. You got this. Whatever school you will end up in next year has no idea how lucky they are. I love you.

Jake. My boy! Whether you want to admit it or not, you're just like me. Lol. I love your confidence (most of the time). Grant looked up to you whether you realized it or not. You were a great example. I pray you have a great year. I love you.

Zack. Our unexpected fourth. What a blessing you have been. You certainly keep us on our toes. You are quite lucky to have three awesome older siblings. You will be our resident IT guy with Jake and Callie away at school. I love you.

I have been truly blessed as a husband and father. I know our whole family still feels a little bit of stress starting a new school year. We were barely a month in last year when Grant had his accident. We all have learned a lot in the last 11 months. We will continue to learn new truths for the rest of our lives. My prayer is that all of the Harrelson's will remember God's goodness and be an example of His grace and love."

Conclusion

It's been almost two years now since Grant's accident. It's been almost a year since my last post. Callie has graduated from Clemson and is starting her first teaching job at Eastside High School. Jake spent this last summer as counselor at Asbury Hills Youth Camp and is starting his junior year at Clemson. Zack has moved up to League Academy for middle school. Kara and I have started talking about retirement. Everyday I am still reminded of those last thirty six hours of Grant's life here on earth. Every Sunday, I look up to my right to the balcony where he used to sit with his friends during worship service. It seems every time I am on the golf course that at some point during the round a cardinal flies by or lands just off the green. Our family made it through his senior season of basketball and prom. We will get through his high school graduation as well. Our family will continue to grieve but will also continue to remember how God has led us through every step of this journey. We have witnessed the full range of not only our emotions but the goodness of God. Our family could not have survived without first and foremost the love and grace of our Savior. Our family, friends, church and community came right along beside us. Their love and support helped keep us afloat. His answer to our prayers was not deliverance from our loss (even though He could've chosen to do so) but a promise to walk with us and transform us so that we can use Grant's death to bring glory to Him. We know that grief is not a destination or a straight line. We know that God will continue to carry us and teach us through this trial until we are reunited with Grant. My prayer is that the words written on these pages would be an encouragement and help to anyone who is going through the pain of grief and loss. The grace and love that God granted to our family is available to all who call on His name. **"Draw near to God and He will draw near to you." James 4:8**

Made in United States
Orlando, FL
23 August 2022

21456471R00039